the Churchyards handbook

the Churchyards handbook

Edited by Thomas Cocke FSA

4th edition

CHURCH HOUSE
PUBLISHING

Church House Publishing
Church House
Great Smith Street
London
SW1P 3NZ

ISBN: 978-0-7151-4301-8

Published 2001 for the Council
for the Care of Churches of the
Church of England by Church
House Publishing.

Copyright © The Archbishops'
Council 2001

Cover design by Visible Edge

Typeset in 9pt Sabon

Printed in England by
Halstan & Co. Ltd
Amersham, Bucks

Contents

List of illustrations

Acknowledgements

A book such as this can only be produced thanks to the hard work
and perseverance of many people. The authors of the different
sections, each experts in their field, deserve especial thanks:
David Harte of the Newcastle Law School for the legal chapters,
Jonathan MacKechnie-Jarvis, Gloucester DAC Secretary, for the
sections on the treatment of cremated remains and commissioning
a memorial, Revd Nigel Cooper, parish priest of Rivenhall,
St Mary the Virgin and a member of Chelmsford DAC, for the
section on the living churchyard. Thanks go also to Dr Christopher
Brooke, an archaeologist and member of Leicester and Southwell
DACs, for drafting the archaeology chapter and writing the guide
to making a churchyard plan and to Chris Hawkings, of the
Ecclesiastical Insurance Group, for the appendix on Health and
Safety.

Thanks are also due to the many people and organizations
who have offered comments on the successive drafts of the text,
especially to Michael Goodman, Chancellor of Guildford Diocese,
the Ecclesiastical Judges Association, Paula Griffiths and Roger
Bowdler of English Heritage, to Harriet Frazer of Memorials by
Artists, to the Commonwealth War Graves Commission and the
National Association of Memorial Masons, as well as to the staff
of Church House Publishing for their help and patience during the
production of the Handbook. Lastly I would like to thank my
colleagues, especially Ingrid Slaughter and Simon Kemp, and my
family for the time they have given to the project.

Thomas Cocke
November 2000

chapter 1
Introduction

The churchyard remains one of the enduring images of this country. Every part of England has these precious places, precious not only because they hold the remains of the departed but also because they embody the history of their community. Nowadays people are becoming aware of the importance not only of the eye-catching features of tombstones and inscriptions but also of the more subtle elements such as the archaeology of churchyard boundaries, the geology of walls and memorials and the ecology of the flora and fauna which churchyards preserve.

In some places the local authority maintains the churchyard. More often it falls to the parish, or rather to a small group who give freely of their time and labour, to keep it green and pleasant. Although this handbook will inevitably address those situations where there are problems, it is important to remember that problems are the exception, not the rule. We can say with pride, rather than with complacency, that in most places the parish tends its churchyard well.

A churchyard is a different place from a local authority cemetery. The purpose of the latter is to provide an appropriate and hygienic service to the inhabitants of the area so that the dead can be interred. Whereas in the nineteenth century a public cemetery was often divided into distinct areas according to denomination, nowadays each plot is assigned without regard to the religious faith, or lack of it, of the deceased. Regulations are made to determine the type of memorial to be erected but these relate to practical issues such as size and safety rather than aesthetic or spiritual ones. Likewise regulations exist to establish maintenance procedures and visiting arrangements, just as they do for any public space. The local authority is rightly agnostic, providing an equal level of facilities to all. In the nineteenth century local authority cemeteries were often planned on a generous scale, with much attention to planting and landscaping. More recent cemeteries are simpler and more economical to run. Local authorities, like parishes, have found the elaborate tombs of the Victorians, and the landscapes, expensive to maintain.

A churchyard is not a neutral space. It is consecrated to its purpose in the name of God, Father, Son and Holy Spirit and, in any works to it, let alone any burials, this special status must be recognized. As with a cemetery, those running a churchyard must pay due attention to health and safety issues and to the convenience of the public, as well as to cost factors, but they must also ensure that whatever is done is in accord with Christian principles. It is for this reason that, while burial in an open Anglican churchyard is a right that can be demanded for anyone who lives within the parish, the burial must be conducted according to the rites and ceremonies of the Church of England.

Burial in a churchyard may in certain circumstances be a right, but commemoration is not. To add something to a churchyard, be it a gravestone, bench or tree, cannot be a private transaction to be agreed informally. It is for the positive purpose of protecting the special status of a churchyard that special rules have to be laid down and observed. The wording of an inscription on a cemetery headstone is a matter for those who erect it, as long as it does not offend public order or decency; that in a churchyard, must have regard for the Christian context in which it is set.

The treatment of a churchyard must be holistic for the same reason. Whereas each plot in a cemetery is the concern of an individual, in a churchyard every element must be kept in due balance so that the total effect, spiritual and aesthetic, speaks a Christian message. Such a message is not to be achieved by crudely erecting texts and crosses but by a combination of the man-made elements with those of the material world. Plants and animals can speak of hope and resurrection.

A similar balance needs to be observed when dealing with the historic features of churchyards. Their archaeology is often complex, involving not only the human remains contained within the churchyard but also evidence from the walls or hedges, the boundary of the churchyard itself as well as any buried structures and, of course, the monuments. There are often scores or even hundreds of monuments of many different styles, periods and materials. While a few may be so important as to warrant listing in their own right, most will be significant as a group. English Heritage and amenity societies, both local and national, are understandably anxious that monuments are preserved but parishes can equally understandably have concerns because of the legal and financial responsibilities they entail.

The Churchyards Handbook was first published in 1962 and this is the third time it has been revised. Each period between revisions has seen great changes in the way society regards churchyards and the religious and cultural issues associated with them but the years since the publication of the last edition in 1988 have witnessed developments of particular significance. Reaction to the tragic death of Princess Diana in 1997 demonstrated that attitudes to death and to the rites of mourning had grown up across the country which were real and powerful but bore little relation to tradition. A growing pluralism and eclecticism in religious beliefs mean that people may be dissatisfied with the set order of service for burials and wish to adapt it, using material that lies remote from the Christian message. The mobility of much of the population has inevitably weakened links within families and any sense of ownership or responsibility for family monuments. Also significant is the way in which the ever-increasing interest in conservation and ecology has changed the perception of churchyards from relics of the past to precious resources for the future. Many of the plants, animals and insects that were once part of the familiar scene, in town and countryside alike, have been driven by development and pollution to find a last refuge in the churchyard.

Perhaps the most complex issue, not only for the Church but for society in general, in approaching the question of how best to regulate burials and graveyards, is that there has been a growing divorce between the legal provisions that have been instituted over the centuries to cover every aspect from sordid to spiritual, and the attitudes of the great majority of people. Few, whatever their social position or religious beliefs, are aware that they may be responsible for maintaining the monuments of their parents and grandparents, let alone more remote ancestors. If people are made more aware of such a responsibility they can confidently repudiate it, knowing that no parish will pursue them in the courts and also that no friend or neighbour would blame them for so doing. Equally, few people have any understanding of the fine distinctions between a parish churchyard open for burials, a closed churchyard in the care of a local authority and a local authority cemetery, and they resent insistence on such distinctions as irrelevant.

Grief and mourning have become largely private matters for individuals, not an experience shared with extended groups of family and community. The way the body of a loved one is treated and remembered is considered a matter of individual preference, rather than subject to generally acknowledged conventions. At the same time, there has been a decided shift towards a freedom of customer choice. In every field of our activity today, the individual is encouraged to shop around to find the product which most closely matches his or her likes and dislikes. The rites of burial and the choice of funerary monuments are no longer considered as belonging to a separate category.

The same trend towards deregulation has affected people's attitude to rules governing matters of taste. The way in which former authors of this handbook were able to insist on certain standards for the design of monuments and for inscriptions upon them might now be thought condescending, rather than authoritative. The reaction of people to any objection to a monument they have chosen can be: 'Why shouldn't we have what we want?', even if, as members of a local history society or an amenity group, the same people might deplore the result as a blot on the land-scape. The free market created by the European Union may in time cause tensions in this area, as firms based on the Continent compete on the British market offering a range of designs for monuments developed for very different aesthetic and religious traditions. If chancellors refuse to sanction such designs, they may be challenged by appeals to the principles of commercial competition or even of human rights.

The graveyard memorial itself is no longer an automatic require-ment, even for regular worshippers. Headstones only began to be common in the late seventeenth century and even so were restricted to the more well-to-do. With the industrialization and greater spread of prosperity of the Victorian era the headstone became virtually universal except for the poorest. Since then the process has reversed. Many families who could well afford a memorial refuse it or prefer to present something useful such as a seat or flower stand instead. Now it is often those on low incomes who insist on gravestones but are understandably anxious not to spend too much on them.

We have learned that the advice in this handbook may need to change with the times. Old-established rules, for instance the absolute resistance to the insertion of photographs on monuments, are being challenged by new techniques. If the image is derived from a photograph but is translated by a computer into direct etching on a stone, it may seem unreasonable to forbid such a technique but to allow similar machine-made rendering of images such as a flower or a cross. If the CCC appeared to insist on the commissioning of original designs by a craftsperson rather than the use of a catalogue, that can be perceived less as encouragement of contemporary skills than as a slur on firms of monumental masons and even as pressure to make people pay more than they need for a headstone.

Tensions are inevitable with so many interlocking interests involved in churchyard matters. Even a seemingly minor question like the length of grass can provoke serious disagreement between those whose mental picture is that of a domestic or municipal lawn and those who prefer a less ordered, meadow look. Should nettles be allowed to grow in the sunny and thus probably prominent sites recommended for the encouragement of butterflies or should the nettles be rooted out as unsightly and potentially painful for children? How do you balance the convenience of tending the area, especially mowing the grass, with the aesthetic and historic interest of features which make the job more time-consuming, like the iron railings once standard to eighteenth- and nineteenth-century tombs or the marble kerbs typical of the early twentieth century? The debate in the latter case is sharpened by the question of money since it can seem prudent to lessen the time and thus cost of mowing by removing every obstacle. It can also be hard to convince sceptics of the value of such features if the railings are rusting or the marble broken.

There is another, more poignant tension between different interests when it comes to the commemoration of cremated remains. For many years, the Council for the Care of Churches as an official body has promoted the practice of allocating a particular area in a churchyard for the interment of cremated remains with just one central memorial to give consolation to mourners, rather than a proliferation of small individual tablets. Alternatively we have encouraged in the place of stone memorials the compilation of a Book of Remembrance to be held in the church to record the names of those whose cremated remains are buried in the churchyard. There is a deep-rooted human desire, however, to give an individual dear to you an individual memorial and to focus on the spot where that person's remains are buried and to identify it with an inscription. From the aesthetic point of view, it is easy to deplore 'postage stamp' tablets dotted about a churchyard, perhaps with dead flowers and jam jars scattered over them, but the mourner will view these things with different eyes.

This edition of the handbook acknowledges differing views rather than laying down prescriptive advice, although this may disappoint those who have used earlier editions to support firm rules. Attitudes to fundamental issues such as mourning rituals and the environment are changing too rapidly for the Council to assume the consensus of views which would enforce them. What the Council can offer in this book is less clear-cut but should prove more useful. From its experience over 80 years of concern for the churchyard and the examples of good practice it has gathered from around the country, it can offer a balanced summary of the principal aspects of the care of churchyards, the legal, the aesthetic, the archaeological, the ecological and of the major issues where uncertainties lie, such as the treatment of cremated remains, the design of memorials and the responsibility for closed churchyards. It is designed as a handbook, not as a set of instructions. The different sections do not pretend to cover every eventuality and exception and in no sense replace specialist texts.

The expert contributors have written in their own style and inevitably overlap from time to time on subjects such as gardens of remembrance. It seems more useful to treat them in the different contexts in which they arise, than to attempt to deal with every aspect in a single reference. Our aim throughout has been to aid all those who either help to regulate and maintain churchyards or wish to know how and why the Church of England addresses the subject. We hope this edition proves in its own way a sound guide over the next decade.

Note to readers

The handbook is aimed primarily at those involved with Anglican churchyards in England. This is not because of denominational or national exclusiveness but simply because of the distinctive legal framework. People in other Churches or other parts of the kingdom are most welcome to make use of whatever sections they find relevant in their own situation.

A concise guide to the good management of your churchyard

- First establish what you have got. Study your churchyard by researching the documentary history and by surveying everything within it, including topographical features and the flora and fauna. Try to illustrate the different elements with photographs taken through the year. Consult local planners and experts, and research at the county record office. Be prepared to pay for professional assistance, e.g. for the survey work and the photographs. It is usually cheaper in the long term to have such things done well than to rely on amateurs.

- Based on these studies, produce a draft management plan for the churchyard and discuss it first within the PCC and the congregation and then with the Parish Council or other secular equivalent. Try to reach agreement on the major elements or at least a workable compromise.

- Publish a user-friendly version of the final plan, expressed in a leaflet or A4 sheet, which tells people both in and outside the congregation about the character of the churchyard and the major features it contains. This explanation will form a natural context for setting out the rules by which the yard is administered. The rules should then be more readily seen as prudent ways of safeguarding an important community asset than an arbitrary imposition from on high.

- Distribute the leaflet as widely as possible, not only to the regular congregation and visitors to the church but also to those living in the neighbourhood, perhaps using the opportunity of Christmas or Easter mailings around the parish. Make sure the leaflet is available in the offices of funerary directors and monumental masons and in local schools.

- Do not rest upon your laurels but put a 'bring forward' date in the parish diary for both leaflet and rules to be considered for revision, perhaps every five years. Meanwhile, whether your church has a yard of particular size or significance or is of only local significance, consider the formation of a group of Friends. Such a group can supply both some extra money for maintenance and also more hands to help. People not otherwise involved with the Church may be willing to join in work parties every month or to conduct tours of the churchyard.

chapter 2

The legal framework

Why law is important for churchyard management

Churchyards have always been significant places for the local
community and thus have had to be regulated by law. An outline
knowledge of this law is essential for anyone involved in the management or care of a churchyard, as well as for anyone concerned
with the burial of a relative. Legal rules can seem complex but their
purpose is to avoid and resolve the problems that can arise.

This handbook can only sketch the main features of the law, so as to
help the reader recognize when and where to turn for professional
advice. Although such advice may seem expensive, it may well save
much money, time and worry in the long run. For general questions,
the diocesan registrar and the archdeacon (or in some circumstances the rural dean) are the most appropriate sources of help.

Churchyards are subject to much of the law that affects land in
general. As the national church, the Church of England can create
law in the form of Measures and Canons. Once Measures have
been voted through the General Synod, Parliament can either
approve or reject, but not amend them. After being approved by
both Houses of Parliament and having received the Royal Assent,
a Measure has the same force as an Act of Parliament.[1] Canons are
made by the General Synod and are primarily directed at regulating
ecclesiastical conduct.

The law is also shaped by the precedents established by cases
decided in both the secular courts and the Church's own
consistory courts, presided over in each diocese by a *chancellor*
who is an experienced lawyer, sometimes a full-time judge in the
secular courts. It is the chancellor who is responsible for approving
or refusing applications for a *faculty*, the legal permit required for
any significant works in church or churchyard. Other bodies, such
as the Diocesan Advisory Committee or English Heritage, have
statutory rights to offer advice but the chancellor retains the
discretion to accept or reject that advice.

The administration of the consistory court is handled by its clerk, the *registrar*. Registrars are solicitors who are retained to advise on ecclesiastical legal matters including the management of church-yards. They can provide guidance on straightforward matters and, if more complex questions arise, can give names of solicitors who can handle cases involving the relevant law. Another important source of help is the Secretary of the Diocesan Advisory Committee for the Care of Churches. The Diocesan Advisory Committee includes clergy, architects and conservation experts and meets regularly to advise the chancellor.[2] A parish should consult the Diocesan Advisory Committee at an early stage before finalizing any proposal of significance relating to a churchyard before opinions become hardened. Such issues are relatively rare. Much more standard are questions from parishioners or the public as to where new burials may take place or what monuments may be erected, in what way the grass should be cut, when the trees may be pruned and who is answerable if someone is injured.

A parish churchyard, along with the church buildings, is normally vested in the incumbent, whether rector or vicar, but responsibility is shared with the Parochial Church Council (the PCC).[3] No significant change either to church or churchyard may be made without a faculty. This applies to every curtilage of a parish church, that is the area belonging to and immediately surrounding the church, whether or not the curtilage has been consecrated as a churchyard[4] by act of the bishop for Christian use. The faculty jurisdiction also extends to land that is not vested in a Church of England body but has been consecrated by the bishop, such as parts of municipal cemeteries and other burial grounds.[5]

Jurisdiction to grant a faculty in straightforward or uncontroversial matters is now delegated to archdeacons, for example repainting a noticeboard or relaying a path.[6] However, authority to allow new churchyard monuments or inscriptions is generally delegated by the chancellor directly to the incumbent or priest-in-charge of each parish, through the issue of diocesan regulations, sometimes termed *rules* or *directions*. These cover the design and materials for a headstone and the wording for inscriptions. Any monument not covered by the diocesan regulations delegating authority to incumbents will require a faculty, as will other works in the churchyard, whether major such as a new hall or extension to the church or more minor, repairing or replacing a boundary wall, erecting a new gate or noticeboard or installing a new drainage system.

Consents and the secular planning system

Quite apart from any need for a faculty, alterations to a churchyard may involve the local planning authority, which will almost always be the district or borough council. Planning permission from the authority will be required for any building or engineering operation, unless it affects only the inside of a building. For example, it will be needed for the erection of a new or replacement structure (such as a wall), for the extension of a church or church hall, for drainage or landscaping works of any consequence, and for relatively minor operations such as laying a new path or altering an existing one. Planning permission will always be required for the creation or extension of a churchyard. The erection of a headstone of standard dimensions is accepted as being outside the scope of planning control, but the erection of a larger monument, such as a new family mausoleum, would require permission. Minor repairs to other structures may not require planning permission, but the planning authority should be notified anyway, particularly where they are of historic interest.

Listed building consent will be required for works, including any significant repairs, to any structure in a churchyard that is listed in its own right, such as a tomb, a lych-gate, or a boundary wall, but not for works to the church itself. For features listed grade 1 or II*, English Heritage must be involved. Conservation area consent will rarely if ever be required, though consent under the Advertisements Regulations (but not planning permission) will sometimes be required for church noticeboards and flagstaffs.

Consultation with the planning authority and any necessary application should be made at the same time as applying for a faculty. Applications may be advertised in the local press and to neighbouring landowners; they may also be given to the parish council. If the authority says that no permission or consent is required, it should be asked to confirm this in writing since failure to obtain planning permission may lead to the issue of an enforcement notice, requiring the works to be undone; failure to obtain listed building consent or advertisements consent, where required, may also lead to criminal prosecution.

Churchyards may also be affected by the Ancient Monuments and Archaeological Areas Act 1979, under which the Secretary of State for Culture, Media and Sport may schedule as an ancient monument 'any building, structure or work, whether above or below the surface of the land or any cave or excavation' that s/he considers to be of national importance.[7] It is an offence to do any work on a scheduled monument without consent from the Secretary of State and 'work' can include dumping material on top of a feature as well as digging into it. An ecclesiastical building in use for ecclesiastical purposes cannot be scheduled as an ancient monument[8] but certain items in a churchyard may be protected by scheduling, including memorials and such features as walls and lych-gates or the footings of a medieval preaching cross. Indeed, an entire churchyard may be scheduled for its archaeological interest, for example where it covers Roman remains.

Archaeological considerations are being given increasing attention in relation to a wide range of works in churchyards, including those standing structures such as charnel houses or boundary walls. New soakaways or other drainage, as well as extensions to church buildings, are likely to be permitted in an ancient churchyard only after careful consideration of the potential archaeological evidence, including a report and, possibly, professional excavation. Because of this sensitivity, it is wise for land near a historic church not to be reused for burials, including interment of cremated remains, unless such use has been checked with the archdeacon and the diocesan archaeological adviser.

A different form of protection may be imposed if part of a churchyard is notified as 'a site of special scientific interest' (SSSI) under the Wildlife and Countryside Act 1981, on the basis of 'flora, fauna or geological or physiographical features'.[9] The effect of this is that certain operations listed in the notice are prohibited unless three months' notice has been given to English Nature (in Wales, the Countryside Commission for Wales). If the site is of national importance, this time may be extended to 18 months.[10] More common are tree preservation orders by the local planning authority.[11]

Visitors, paths and rights of way

Because the Church of England is established as the national church, it holds its buildings and land, including its parish churchyards, as steward, not simply for local worshippers, but for the public at large. All people residing within the parish have significant legal rights relating mainly to burial, as do those dying there, even if they were not residents.

The right of the public to visit a particular churchyard is not as straightforward as it may seem since they have no general right of access.[12] There probably will be a customary right of access for parishioners, especially where the churchyard has existed for many centuries and such parishioners' access may in practice be difficult to distinguish from a right enjoyed by the general public. There may also be an ancient footpath that entitles the general public to cross a churchyard. Such paths should be shown as rights of way on the definitive map of public rights of way that is maintained by each local authority.[13] Problems may arise about the use of paths over which public rights are claimed where the PCC wishes to keep people out of a churchyard, especially at night for security reasons, or to restrict use, for example where a path runs beside a tower or a boundary wall that has become dangerous. There are statutory procedures available through local authorities or the magistrates' courts for closing or diverting a right of way or for temporarily restricting its use.[14] These procedures can be difficult and may be unnecessary, if it can be demonstrated that there is no legal basis for the right.

Normally, a way which has been enjoyed by the public as of right for twenty years is deemed to have been dedicated as a highway, unless there is sufficient evidence that there was no intention during that period to dedicate it.[15] However, although churchyard paths may physically be laid out for public use under faculty, they do not become permanent public rights of way. Even if such paths are shown on a definitive map, it may be possible to have them removed. It is prudent to challenge any proposal to make a new entry on a definitive map showing a public path across a churchyard. To avoid any possible dispute footpaths should be closed one day in the year, or a notice should be exhibited in the churchyard making clear that entry is granted as a matter of grace by the church authorities.

If a parish wants to change the layout of a churchyard or to put down paths, a faculty will be necessary. Normally such changes will be for the benefit of the local church, of visiting parishioners and of members of the public. A path or a road may also be laid so as to provide a better access to private property nearby.[16] The faculty authorizing this may be granted along with a licence to use the access for a set period of time, perhaps 30 or 99 years. Similarly, a faculty may be granted for the installation of underground services, such as water mains or electricity cables or of lamp-posts or posts for telephone wires or a communications aerial.[17] Such installations may provide a valuable service and help to raise revenue for maintenance but these benefits must be weighed against any visual intrusion.

Sometimes problems arise concerning access to a churchyard. Where glebe or part of the parsonage land near the churchyard is sold off, it is important for future access to the church and to the churchyard to be safeguarded. For example, road traffic past the usual church entrance may increase, making it desirable to create a new access from another direction. Although sales of glebe and other parish land are now effectively made by the diocese, subject to the approval of the Church Commissioners,[18] it is people at parish level, such as churchwardens and PCC members, who are most aware of likely future needs and so must make sure that the decision-makers allow adequate provision for future access.

Problems may arise if adequate rights have not been preserved in earlier sales. A property crossed by an access route to a churchyard may have an unsympathetic new owner,[19] or disputes can arise between the owner and the incumbent which are complex and pastorally damaging. It is vital that legal advice should be sought through the diocese to resolve them as soon as possible. Such problems also serve as a reminder of the caution that needs to be exercised in any such sales. They may raise revenue for one generation, but the land in question may be crucial in providing necessary facilities in the future.

Boundaries

The PCC has an obligation to ensure that the churchyard boundary is 'duly fenced'.[20] In practice, the 'fence' will commonly be a wall. The duty is concerned with ensuring the sacred character of the churchyard, rather than making it impenetrable to intruders. Where a boundary wall becomes dangerous and is likely to fall onto neighbouring property, it will be regarded as a legal nuisance and the PCC will be under an obligation to repair it. If it does fall and causes damage, the PCC will be liable to pay compensation. If a wall falls onto a highway and causes injury to a passer-by or to any property, such as a parked car, the PCC will be liable, even where it had no reason to suspect danger. There are only limited exceptions as, for example, where a vandal or other unknown person has secretly made the wall unsafe or where there is some latent defect that could not have been discovered, as where the foundations have been washed away by a burst water main.[21]

No part of the churchyard can be alienated, even under a faculty,[22] except by statutory procedures, such as compulsory purchase or a pastoral scheme. Although a person may acquire a piece of neighbouring private land by treating it as their own for twelve years, for example by moving a fence so as to extend a garden into part of another garden next door,[23] any part of a churchyard treated in this way would be of little value to the person who acquired it, because it would retain its status as consecrated land subject to the faculty jurisdiction.

Health and safety (see also Appendix 2)

Those responsible for a churchyard have a constant responsibility to carry out necessary maintenance to prevent accidents to visitors. As well as making sure that boundary walls are safe, PCCs should keep a watchful eye for any potentially dangerous trees, grave-stones or other hazards. Obvious hazards may be mentioned in the quinquennial report on the church and churchyard which must be obtained from a surveyor or architect.[24] Since the incumbent and the PCC will normally share control over the churchyard and will therefore be treated as joint occupiers,[25] they will owe a duty to visitors under the Occupiers' Liability Act 1957. Even within a closed churchyard where maintenance has been transferred to the local authority and it has become occupier, the PCC and the incumbent may continue to share responsibility. For example, they may be left to clear paths of snow or to sprinkle sand when the weather is frosty and they may also continue to be responsible for such potential dangers as loose manhole covers. In the case of potentially dangerous memorials, the heirs at law of the person commemorated may be liable and, if they can be located, should be approached to pay for remedial work before any accident can occur.

An occupier of land must take reasonable care for the safety of visitors and their belongings for the purpose for which they are on the land.[26] What is reasonable varies with the circumstances; particular care must be taken to protect children, whereas persons employed to do a particular job may be expected to take more precautions on their own part. If there is a dangerous wall or headstone where children may be expected to play, it will be important to fence it off securely or to take other steps to keep children away. However, even a mason called in to repair a source of danger must be told of any risk known to the church authorities, especially if it is not obvious, such as the fractured cover to a vault.

There is now a duty, under the Occupiers' Liability Act 1984, to take reasonable care even for the safety of trespassers who may enter the churchyard when it is locked at night. If a newly dug grave were left overnight beside an unlit path, or a scythe were left lying on the path, a person who was injured using the path could probably recover compensation, whether it was a parishioner coming to tend a grave or a thief seeking to break into the church. Similarly, a duty would also be owed to a drunken reveller misbehaving in the churchyard, although, if such a person were injured, a court might well take the view that the real cause of the accident was the failure by the victim to take reasonable care for his or her own safety. The duty owed by an occupier to trespassers is met, according to the Act, 'by taking such steps as are reasonable in all the circumstances of the case to give warning of the danger concerned or to discourage persons from incurring the risk'.[27]

The PCC needs to guard against liability by taking out adequate insurance to meet its responsibilities as a corporate body, charged not only with keeping the churchyard duly fenced but also with ensuring that the churchyard itself is kept in 'an orderly and decent manner as becomes consecrated ground'.[28] The incumbent and the PCC will be expected to recognize obvious dangers, such as loose slates on the roof above a path or a rotten tree over an area with regularly visited graves, and to take steps to ensure that no harm arises.

An individual PCC member could be personally liable if he or she became aware of a danger and failed to report it. Alternatively someone cutting grass in the churchyard may cause injury through carelessness and so will be liable to the person injured. The incumbent or PCC may also be liable if they allow the danger to occur through inadequate supervision, for example if scything were allowed when children were playing nearby.

If a person who negligently injures someone else while working in the churchyard is regularly employed by the PCC, the PCC will be responsible under the principle of vicarious liability. This does not usually apply where an accident is caused by someone doing work for the PCC as a contractor, such as a builder putting in drains, or by a person permitted to carry out work for themselves or for someone else, as where a monumental mason erects a tombstone. The PCC and the incumbent may become liable if they fail to intervene where it is apparent that such work is not being done safely, e.g. where they know that a danger has been created as a result of bad workmanship but they fail to sort out the problem by insisting that the work be redone. In the meantime, if there is danger, appropriate warning notices or fencing must be put up. In the particular case of work carried out next to the highway such as repairing a dangerous wall, the PCC as employer will be strictly liable for any negligence, even where the work is carried out by an independent contractor.[29]

Abuse of the churchyard

Churchyards can be vulnerable to deliberate abuse, whether in the form of vandalism or rowdyism or even as targets for macabre behaviour such as black magic rituals.[30] Not only is such behaviour particularly offensive to the congregation and to the relatives and friends of those whose remains are buried there, but even those without explicit Christian beliefs will be upset if burial places are treated with disrespect. Here the criminal law may serve as a valuable safeguard.

chapter 3

Graves and the interment of cremated remains

The right to burial

Historically, the churchyard was the burial place for every resident within a parish. Nowadays the secular local authorities have a legal duty to provide for the disposal of bodies where no one else has made suitable arrangements[1] and there will therefore be a municipal cemetery which will normally be owned and run by the district council overseeing the parish[2] whether within or at some distance from the parish. Nevertheless, so long as there is an open churchyard in the parish, i.e. a churchyard which has not been formally closed by an Order of the Privy Council on the grounds that there is no longer space available for burials, anyone who dies in the parish or while resident in it is entitled to burial there. Thus there is a right of burial for persons who have no previous connection but happen to die in the parish, for example in a road accident, or for those who die out of the parish but regarded it as their home. These rights apply to anyone, irrespective of whether they had any church or Christian commitment. There is also a right of burial for anyone who died while on the electoral roll of a parish having an open churchyard,[3] regardless of where they reside or die.[4]

If there is sufficient room, a discretion to permit burial for persons without formal rights is allowed to incumbents or other appointed clerics.[5] (If there is no priest-in-charge or experienced assistant curate, the rural dean is likely to be responsible for making such decisions.) A typical case would be where the deceased had lived in the parish for many years but had moved away when elderly, to live near family members or in sheltered accommodation, or where the deceased had regularly spent holidays in the parish and had been actively involved with the parish church.

If space seems to be becoming limited, the incumbent and the PCC[6] should combine to agree a parochial policy, especially as the former is required to take account of any general guidance which the PCC may give on this matter.[7] It will be wise to seek advice from the archdeacon over long-term plans, particularly any involving substantial changes to the use of the churchyard which will require a faculty, such as setting aside an area for cremated remains.

Even where there is a right to burial in a particular churchyard, the incumbent or other relevant person is entitled to designate the place for the grave, unless a space has already been reserved by faculty.[8] Similarly, the incumbent may specify the depth of the grave. There is no standard depth, but various Orders in Council and local Acts and by-laws may require a specific depth of soil above a coffin, which may vary from as little as 0.6 m (2 ft) to as much as 1.5 m (5 ft). In urban churchyards, the Town Improvement Clauses Act 1847 which stipulates at least 0.75 m (30 in) may have been incorporated into a local Act.[9]

The incumbent also has discretion as to the materials of the coffin, for instance to refuse permission for a metal or stone coffin. He or she might for ecological reasons want to go further and to encourage burials without a coffin or in a readily biodegradable container. Any unusual policy of this sort should be introduced only with the full agreement of the PCC.

If archaeological remains are found while a grave is being dug in a part of the churchyard where there are no other recent burials, it may be wise to choose a new site for graves. Such considerations may also affect the depth of graves.

Burial rights and the reservation of grave spaces

A grave can only be reserved in a particular place after a petition for a faculty, usually by the family, has been granted by the chancellor, not after an informal promise by an incumbent. The faculty will normally be subject to a condition requiring a suitable sum to be paid to the incumbent and/or into the churchyard maintenance fund of the church concerned. Such a faculty is commonly granted where a husband or wife wishes to have a space reserved next to a spouse who has already been interred or where children wish to be interred near their parents. No right to a particular space will be granted unless the chancellor considers it appropriate. Once a faculty is obtained, it must be recorded so that there can be no risk that the space will be used for anyone else. There have been harrowing incidents when remains that have been wrongly interred in a space reserved for someone else have had to be removed.[10] It is equally important to remind applicants that the reservation of a grave space does not carry with it any associated right to erect a monument.

A faculty reserving a burial space will normally relate to a particular individual or individuals and cannot be transferred even to another member of the family except under a new faculty. If a person for whom a space has been reserved no longer requires it, perhaps because he or she has already been buried elsewhere, a new faculty should be obtained for the burial of someone else and it would be prudent, to prevent misunderstanding, for the incumbent to check the wishes of any family having an interest in the space and in any remains already buried there.

More extensive private burial rights may exist over land that has been added to a consecrated churchyard. Anyone who gives such land may reserve private burial rights, including the right to erect monuments, in perpetuity, in up to one sixth of the land given. These rights are private property that may be passed on or sold, although they may be used only for persons who would in any event be entitled to burial in consecrated ground.[11]

The Faculty Jurisdiction Measure 1964 (Section 8) provided that any existing burial rights would cease 100 years after the passing of the Measure and that any future burial rights granted by faculty should not be for more than 100 years. In any case a reservation only needs to be continued until a date by which the person to be buried is bound to have died. A burial right may be extended but, equally, once a reserved space has been used, there is no bar on its being used again after a reasonable period, at the incumbent's discretion, and subject to parochial policy. A common time limit for the reuse of grave spaces is 50 years, which is the normal minimum time since the latest interment after which a burial ground may be cleared under statutory powers allowing redevelopment of the land (Chapter 6). At present (2001) there is a growing interest in reopening closed churchyards for burial which may stimulate changes in the law.

Interment of cremated remains

Nowadays most people in England and Wales are cremated. Many who are entitled to be buried in a parish churchyard choose instead for their cremated remains to be interred there. Indeed this is generally so when cremation follows a Church of England funeral service.[12] Someone who has a right to burial in a churchyard or other parish burial ground will also have a right of burial there for their cremated remains.[13] As with any burial, the incumbent will designate the site, unless there is a place reserved by faculty. The common practice is for the chancellor to approve local rules made by the PCC to deal with cremated remains and to set aside a special area by faculty for their interment.

Where a church does not have a churchyard but does have a suitable curtilage, i.e. an area of open ground within its boundary, it can apply for a faculty to landscape the area and to use it for the interment of cremated remains. In such a case the bishop should be approached to consecrate the area.

Burials within church buildings have generally not been permitted for many years[14] but it is sometimes appropriate in special cases, such as that of a long-serving incumbent, to deposit cremated remains under the floors, never in the walls, of a church.[15] A faculty must be obtained for any such interments. A church architect must ensure they do not interfere with heating or lighting ducts, and an archaeologist recognized by the diocese must confirm that they will not disturb archaeological deposits. It may prove possible to place the remains within a disused vault.

Methods of interment of cremated remains in a churchyard

The common practice of referring to cremated remains as 'ashes' is not strictly accurate. In fact they consist of calcined bone that has been purified by fire and ground down. To bury them, the recommended practice is to commit them directly to the earth by pouring them into a suitably prepared hole and immediately covering them with soil. Further practical advice is given later in the chapter on the treatment of cremated remains.

On occasion it may be possible even in a closed churchyard to use a grave space granted previously by faculty[16] or to obtain a licence from the Home Office to revive an old right so as to allow for a new burial. In such cases, the right may also be claimed for cremated remains. It is more frequent for the clergy to allow the interment of cremated remains in a closed churchyard, particularly in the grave of a relative, although this can only be done if a general or specific faculty has been granted. It may be preferable to obtain a faculty to set aside an area for burial of cremated remains[17] but if a local authority has taken over responsibility for managing that churchyard, it should always be consulted first before any area is set aside for cremated remains and should be cited on the presentation of the petition seeking the necessary faculty.[18] The faculty should make clear whose remains are to be allowed and how far interment will be a matter of right or within the discretion of the incumbent, as well as the boundaries of the area and any arrangements for landscaping and monuments.

A grave space reserved or used for the burial of an individual in either an open or a closed churchyard can be subsequently used for interring cremated remains, perhaps those of several members of the same family. This should be planned in advance so that earlier interments are made at a greater depth. The question of a memorial should also be settled in advance by obtaining a general faculty for the area, or a specific faculty. In many dioceses the incumbent is authorized to allow an addition to an existing inscription.

Exhumation

Human remains once interred in a churchyard should not be disturbed, save for good reason. The coroner may order exhumation if any question arises as to the circumstances of death.[19] Otherwise a faculty will always be necessary and, in addition, unless the remains are to be reinterred in consecrated ground, a Home Office licence.[20] Exhumation is most likely to be requested where works are to be carried out, whether for the church, such as an extension, or for essential secular purposes such as a road widening scheme, or, if the churchyard is made redundant, under a pastoral scheme. In such cases the practical advantages must be balanced against respect due to the deceased.

There are occasions when relatives ask permission for remains to be removed. They must show that there is 'a good and proper reason for exhumation, that reason being likely to be regarded as acceptable by right thinking members of the Church at large'.[21] Permission may then be granted in exceptional cases, for example where, soon after interment, it becomes clear that executors have overlooked a clear direction in a will that the deceased should be interred in another place. In general, such exhumation is distressing to all concerned and is strongly discouraged. It will not be permitted, for example, where a surviving spouse moves and is unable to continue visiting the grave regularly.[22] The case of cremated remains is treated with the same caution as other burials, especially as subsequent removal will normally be out of the question for practical reasons.[23]

chapter 4
Monuments

The most striking feature of any churchyard is likely to be the monuments, whether these are elaborate chest tombs or simple headstones. Monuments are a solace to the relatives of the people they commemorate; visitors come to look at them and passers-by pause to read. They embody the social history of a community and form a tangible expression of its roots. Most important, they express the purpose of the churchyard, as a place where the mortal remains of past generations of Christian people are reverently laid and their earthly lives recorded.

The law regulating what monuments may be erected, and also what may happen to them later, has important implications for Christian ministry. Regrettably, monuments can sometimes cause dissension or misunderstanding, particularly where relatives are not allowed to erect the type of stone or to have carved the inscription that they have chosen. The designs proposed may not only lack aesthetic distinction but take little account of the essentially Christian nature of a churchyard. On the other hand, it may be pastorally difficult to refuse an unsatisfactory memorial if that is likely to cause resentment and distress.

Monuments are also of concern for historical and artistic reasons and because of the pleasure that they give to the public. Conservation societies and individual enthusiasts expect protection for the settings of ancient churches and a high quality for any additions. This may conflict with the pastoral need to accord with the individual wishes of the bereaved, especially where a person being commemorated had a real connection with the church.

Until the nineteenth century, monuments were affordable for only a small proportion of burials. Today, a mass-produced gravestone is commonly provided as part of the service offered by funeral directors. The material used may well be out of keeping with the churchyard for which it is intended, since the firm providing the stone may be based many miles away and have no established relationship with the parish or its incumbent. It is therefore a vital responsibility of incumbents and of others who have the charge of parish churchyards to make sure that the legal requirements for a particular diocese are clearly but sensitively explained and enforced. A copy of the diocesan churchyard regulations should be sent to all undertakers and monumental masons operating in the area.

Probably the single most important principle in erecting a memorial in a churchyard is that it should not be done too soon. Good practice and good sense suggest a delay of at least six months after the burial. This allows time for the grave to settle and time for pastoral advice from the incumbent as to an acceptable type of monument and inscription. In any event, a grave mound will need to be levelled after six months to allow for grass cutting.

The right to erect a monument

There is no general right for anyone to put up a memorial in a churchyard or to add an inscription to an existing memorial. Appropriate permission must always be obtained first. Church authorities are sometimes criticized for being petty or unfeeling where bereaved relatives are not allowed to erect a monument that they have chosen. However, a burial space is not a piece of private property but forms part of an area in which the community at large has a strong interest. A policy controlling memorials must take account of the feelings of people whose relatives are already buried nearby or who may themselves be buried there in due time, and also the wider planning and conservation issues. The Church operates its own control system so that it can balance different priorities of this kind and must exercise the system effectively if it is to be credible.

Monuments that do not comply with the diocesan churchyard regulations will require a faculty, to be granted only after all the relevant procedures have been completed and the payment of a fee. The terms of formal approval must be followed exactly with regard to the details of materials, design and inscription. Permission granted by an incumbent will also create a right to erect a monument, but only if the permission is within the power delegated by the chancellor and if it does not interfere with existing rights. Thus, a relative who puts up an over-large tomb with the vicar's permission might have to remove it, as the vicar's delegated power would not cover such a construction. Similarly, permission would be ineffective if it were given for a monument that partly covered a neighbouring grave where someone else already had a place reserved by an earlier faculty, perhaps to allow a burial next to a husband or wife whose remains were already there.[1] If a monument is wrongly erected a faculty will then be necessary for its removal. In a blatant case of carelessness or where the law was wilfully disregarded, the incumbent or anyone else involved could be liable to pay the costs of removing a memorial[2] and of the necessary faculty proceedings.[3]

Like incumbents, all those who are professionally concerned with burials and with memorials have a clear duty to comply with the relevant law.[4] Regrettably, abuse does sometimes occur and then the powers of the court to order restoration may be used, for example against a firm of monumental masons. In an extreme case the consistory court can even invoke the help of the High Court to deal with an offender by means of contempt proceedings.[5]

Funeral companies should resist offering package deals for funerals which include any monument for erection in a churchyard. Neither should they give bereaved persons a catalogue of designs for memorials that are unlikely to be regarded as suitable in a church-yard. It should always be made clear to clients that the form of a memorial and any inscription must take account of the legal restrictions governing materials and designs in that particular parish, if approval is to be granted.

The approval process

Although the diocesan chancellor has the ultimate authority to allow a new memorial or an addition to an inscription, in straightforward cases he or she will transfer this power to incumbents by regulations in a signed instrument of delegation. The instrument only allows incumbents to authorize certain types of memorial. Applications to the incumbent for a memorial that seems to belong to this non-contentious category should always be in writing, using a standard form accompanied by a clear drawing showing dimensions, materials, inscriptions and the like. Incumbents and the diocesan registrar should hold a stock of such forms.

Anyone wishing to erect a monument that is outside an incumbent's delegated authority may petition the chancellor to grant a faculty. A careful design by an able artist is likely to be looked on favourably. In such a case, the Diocesan Advisory Committee must be consulted before the chancellor makes a decision on the application.[6]

A petition for a faculty should be made by the executor, other personal representative, or by a close relative of the person to be commemorated, so as to ensure he or she has legal standing. Where there is a will, the executor's authority dates from the moment of death, but in the approval of a memorial, other interested parties may have to be considered. Problems may occur if there are family disagreements,[7] for example between children of the person commemorated or between a legal spouse and someone else who was living with the deceased at the time of death.

Regulations on materials, size and design

Churchyard regulations are now established for every diocese and are available from the diocesan office and the registrar. The CCC holds a collection of them. It is thus no longer appropriate to propose model regulations, as in previous editions of this handbook. Anyone wishing to know what is permitted in a particular churchyard should not only obtain an up-to-date copy of the diocesan regulations but also check with the incumbent whether any special regulations apply. Thus, while diocesan rules may provide that memorials authorized by incumbents must normally be of local stone or of unpolished granite, an incumbent and PCC, with the approval of the chancellor, may decide to restrict even unpolished granite to a section of the churchyard away from the church and masked by a hedge.

Inevitably churchyard regulations will sometimes be seen as negative and obstructive. However, when they work properly, they enable both the bereaved and the Church to conduct their affairs more easily. The delay they involve before any memorial may be approved provides a valuable opportunity to reflect and to choose a worthy design and materials. The need to discuss suitable words for an inscription may even help the grieving process. Although there are no standard regulations throughout the Church of

England, this chapter outlines the general approach to memorials and inscriptions adopted by chancellors.

One of the areas where regulations give rise to problems relates to mass-produced designs, using materials which, though readily available, lack local character. Where some memorials have already been put up which are out of keeping with the church building and with older monuments, it may be difficult to draw the line so as to forbid any more. Those who would like to put up a new memorial should be warned that their proposal will not necessarily be permitted, even if it is similar to certain monuments put up in the past.

Choices of materials and design are too often regarded as purely subjective questions. Those involved with the design of a new building or a monument can generally come to an agreed solution, if the proposal is essentially in keeping with what is there already. There is likely to be more dispute when the proposal is clearly different and opinion is divided as to whether it makes a satisfying contrast or an unpleasant clash. Many people feel that a church-yard is not an appropriate setting for modern materials, such as concrete, glass, steel or plastic, especially as they do not weather attractively. There is, however, much opportunity for imaginative contemporary designs, using traditional organic materials such as stone or wood.

The power delegated to incumbents usually states limits to the size of a grave marker. The National Association of Memorial Masons recommends the following dimensions: between 750 mm (2 ft 6 in) and 1200 mm (4 ft) high; between 500 mm (1 ft 8 in) and 900 mm (3 ft) wide; and between 75 mm (3 in) and 150 mm (6 in) thick. Slate memorials may be thinner, at 38 mm (1½ in). Another regular exception is made for graves of the Commonwealth War Graves Commission, which have their own standard of 801 mm (2 ft 8 in) high by 372 mm (1 ft 3 in) broad.

Stones need to be fixed securely, ensuring that the memorial is stable, allowing for the type of soil and the possibility of settlement. They should not have unsightly bases that can damage mowing machines. If a base is allowed it should be made of stone, like the memorial itself, and project no further than 100 mm (4 in) beyond the stone above in any direction. If diocesan regulations allow the base to incorporate a flower receptacle, it is common to allow a larger projection of up to 200 mm (8 in) with the receptacle flush with the top of the base.

Shapes that may be common in municipal cemeteries, such as a heart or open book, have been discouraged by Church authorities as alien to the churchyard setting and as liable to be trivialized by repetition. An even firmer line has been taken against the incorporation of photographs in a memorial, common enough abroad but not part of the British tradition. For one thing, the climate tends to cause the deterioration of both frame and photograph. However, the recent development of etching computer-generated images from photographs direct on to the stone has created a rather different situation. Maintenance considerations mean that features such as kerb stones, chippings and glass shades are also discouraged.

It must be admitted that efforts to avoid the restless and discordant effect of inappropriately shaped and sized stones can result in uniform rows of very similar headstones, lacking the character of earlier memorials. There is much to be said for encouraging variety, as long as the emphasis remains on quality.

Whether a design that is not covered by the range delegated to incumbents will prove acceptable depends on the discretion of the particular chancellor, acting on the advice of the Diocesan Advisory Committee, and the individual circumstances of the case. Figurative sculpture of the Victorian variety may be judged unfashionable and costly compared to other forms of sculpture. A traditional stone can be enlivened by relief carving on the surface or inset with a bronze plaque creating an object of artistic merit without overmuch expense. The guiding principles should be that new designs are made to a high standard and that what they depict is consistent with Christian belief and the character of the particular churchyard. The new memorial should in future form a worthy part of the churchyard heritage.

Previous editions of this handbook advised that the cross, the supreme Christian symbol, should not have its impact weakened by overuse. Others consider that the cross is the most suitable memorial on a Christian grave. There are also practical considerations.

Free-standing stone crosses need to be particularly well designed and constructed. They are liable to vandalism or accidental damage and when broken can look unsightly. It may be wiser as well as more appropriate to erect a cross of wood, but again the quality of the timber and of the design should be truly worthy of their purpose.

Inscriptions

The question of inscriptions on memorials can prove even more contentious than the choice of materials or design.[8] Both the content of an inscription and the standard of lettering are important. Later additions made to an inscription should be consistent with the original, in size, style and quality of execution and require specific approval. Incumbents may be authorized to allow relief inscriptions as well as incised ones, and to permit the painting of incised inscriptions, but not letters made of plastic or other inserted substances. A modest trademark of no more than 13 mm (^{1}/$_2$ in) may be permitted in the side or on the back of a stone.

Chancellors generally authorize incumbents to approve wording that is 'simple and reverent', for instance appropriate quotations from the Bible and other literary sources. Parish regulations should be used to set out local policies in this area which can then be followed consistently.

The theological implications of an inscription are important but the issues of social usage can prove even more controversial. The use of familiar or colloquial terms on memorials raises strong feelings. For many, the description of someone as 'A devoted and much loved dad and granddad' is the natural expression of the feelings he evoked in life; for others such language is overfamiliar for what is a public statement. Diocesan chancellors, or indeed individual parishes, subject to the approval of the chancellor, are free to make their own policies and to temper them to meet local and individual needs. Restrictions in a particular parish on the use of familiar terms should only be introduced after open discussion in the PCC and should be reconsidered at regular intervals. It must be acknowledged that in all areas of life, informal modes are becoming preferred to formal. Maintaining the standards of earlier years can be misinterpreted as snobbery or insensitivity. It is vital that any restrictions are imposed consistently. A practice may be forbidden in one particular churchyard, even if it is permitted elsewhere in the diocese, but any exception will seem unfair to those who have previously been denied it.[9] It is similarly embarrassing if practice varies greatly between neighbouring parishes or dioceses, whether concerning inscriptions or other details such as the use of gilded lettering. The only answer is to inform and educate the community, both within the congregation and outside, as to why restrictions are desirable.

Memorials in respect of cremated remains

The practice of cremation has continued to grow but its implications for the traditional churchyard are still being worked out. In earlier editions of this handbook, various suggestions were made for appropriate memorials in respect of cremated remains but no one type or style has become established. Christian teaching emphasizes the dignity of the human body which should be treated with respect even after death. The bereaved are generally anxious that the remains of loved ones should be treated properly. They often also feel a deep need to honour the specific place where the remains are laid as particularly associated with the departed. For such people it is not enough to know that ashes have been deposited in a churchyard but they want to go to the particular spot where the ashes are interred.

In a churchyard that is still in use, it is now normal for an area to be set aside by faculty for cremated remains. The choice of such an area needs to be made with particular sensitivity. It must be not only attractive but protected from interruption from passers-by. On the other hand to select a secluded part of the churchyard may be unwise from the security point of view.

As with burials of bodies, there is no right to provide a memorial in respect of cremated remains but permission to do so may be obtained by faculty from the chancellor or through delegated power from the incumbent. However, some dioceses as a matter of policy do not allow individual memorials for cremated remains and restrict commemoration to an entry in a Book of Remembrance. When cremated remains are interred in the existing grave of a relative, an appropriate addition to the inscription may be authorized.

Where the churchyard is closed for burials so that the incumbent normally has no responsibility for approving memorials, particular care has to be taken to ensure that any addition to an existing inscription is suitably worded and executed.

In practice, it has proved difficult to satisfy the desire of the bereaved for a lasting and tangible memorial at the chosen place where cremated remains have been interred. Past schemes providing a designated area for cremated remains have often authorized the incumbent to approve modest tablets of specified size and materials. However, a scaled-down memorial that is proportional in size to individual cremated remains is inherently unsatisfying. The tendency has often been to set small stones flush with the ground, bearing minimal inscriptions, which can soon become indecipherable and uneven. Individual plaques of this sort may produce a patch-work appearance, particularly unattractive if the area for cremated remains is close to the church.

Other schemes provide for a paved area. In cities or in certain parts of the country, such as Yorkshire or Lancashire, there are ancient paved churchyards, but extensive areas of this sort require coherently laid stones of adequate size and may create rather an oppressive effect. It is more common, and likely to be more satis-factory, to lay memorial stones so as to form an edging to a path or to make up the path itself. Another method of commemoration is to incorporate tablets in a wall. If tablets are set into an existing wall, especially an ancient wall, care must be taken not to damage it. It may be preferable to construct a new wall with memorial inscriptions on the individual stones of which it is composed. As always with stone memorials, account may need to be taken of the risk of vandalism and theft.

The Council's advice in earlier editions of this handbook was that stones used to mark cremated remains should only be authorized for a set period, such as 25 years. After that time they could be removed or turned over for reuse, unless permission had been obtained for them to remain longer. This arrangement seems to have been followed successfully in a number of dioceses. Other approaches have included the provision of a columbarium, a struc-ture in which the ashes can be placed in a kind of locker which is then sealed by the inscribed stone. A columbarium can be either purpose-built or created in an existing funerary vault. The advantage of a columbarium is that it may meet the demand for the disposal of cremated remains for a long time ahead. As discussed earlier, a faculty may be obtained occasionally for the interment of cremated remains under the floor of a church, where the person concerned has made some exceptional contribution to the life of the Church or of the community.

One attractive alternative to individual memorials on the site of interment is a Book of Remembrance kept in the church. This is considered further in the later chapter on the treatment of cremated remains. One major reason why such books have not become established as a more common form of memorial is the difficulty of access, as church buildings are often shut for security reasons, except for services. The importance and also the problems of keeping church buildings open as much as possible are beyond the scope of this handbook. However, if Books of Remembrance are used, it is vital to allow people inside the church and make them more aware of it as a place of worship and of welcome. Two further advantages of an entry in a Book of Remembrance over a small individual memorial are the scope for giving more information about the deceased, and the greater durability of such a volume. Individual memorials in the churchyard are likely to have little room for a meaningful inscription and they may well be removed after a number of years.

Other ways of encouraging the use of a Book of Remembrance are to develop liturgical opportunities, such as a new emphasis on the festivals of All Souls and All Saints, or to use the book to focus thoughts on those who have died on a particular day of the year. The pages may then be turned so that they are open for the relevant date.

Because the book will need to be protected in a locked case, casual visitors will be frustrated if they want to read a particular entry. It is important that a copy of the whole book, properly presented on durable paper and in a good cover, should be available for visitors to examine. The copy should be securely fixed, perhaps chained, in or near the case that houses the original book.

chapter 5
Maintenance and management

This chapter deals with three subjects. First, it is essential to maintain a full and up-to-date record, not only of memorials but of other features and of plants in the churchyard and of any changes that take place. Second, and equally important, there should be clear arrangements for maintenance to ensure that the churchyard is kept safe and in order. Third, and perhaps the most common headache, is the need to make adequate financial provision for such maintenance.

Like church buildings and congregations, parish churchyards vary greatly in character. The law sets down some basic principles on how churchyards are to be run but, within these, chancellors may lay down more detailed rules varying from diocese to diocese. The regular maintenance of any churchyard is inescapably the responsibility of the parish, which effectively means the PCC.[1] How maintenance is carried out will depend on parish resources, on the priorities of the incumbent and on the initiative of volunteers.

PCCs can manage churchyards in a wide variety of ways beyond simply keeping them safe and tidy. A prudent PCC will set aside time to review its churchyard policy every few years, identifying what purposes the churchyard serves and to consider whether adaptation is needed. A parish church with a large churchyard and a small congregation may regard the churchyard as a burden. A thriving parish with a busy programme of evangelism may regard it as an irrelevance. However, the churchyard can provide a means of involving people who find direct involvement with the worship of the church off-putting. Tending a relative's grave or being able to sit on a bench and eat lunchtime sandwiches may lead to helping with the upkeep of the churchyard and perhaps, in time, joining the congregation.

Registers and records

In every area of church life, just as elsewhere, there are extensive and growing duties to keep records.[2] Often these demands seem

burdensome because their purpose is not made clear. The requirement for the Church of England to maintain a wide range of
records is a result of the essentially public nature of Christianity in
England. Where the public have rights, as they do with respect to
church services and burial, they must generally have access to any
relevant information. In the case of burials, there are obvious
reasons for ensuring accurate records, to avoid conflicts or distress
where other interments take place nearby and in exceptional but
vital cases to allow for investigations by the police and other
public officials. Burial registers are formally owned by the PCC[3]
but are in the custody of the incumbent[4] or, during a vacancy, of
the churchwardens.[5]

There is a legal requirement for each parish to maintain a record of
burials which take place in the churchyard including disposals of
cremated remains,[6] though a separate register should be kept for the
latter. Both records should list the same information: the full name of
the deceased; his or her age and former home address; the date and
location of burial; the name of the officiating minister.[7] In addition,
the register of interments of cremated remains should record any
funeral service and the place of cremation preceding the interment.

A major reason for recent increases in the requirements of record
keeping is the established status of the Church of England, entrusted
with protecting a substantial proportion of the national heritage.
Churchyard memorials, like other features in churchyards, are
parts of that heritage which require to be recorded and monitored.
Such tasks may seem a distraction from the main work of the
Church but may also be taken as an opportunity. Well recorded
and presented churchyards can draw visitors and can help to show
the Church as a responsible and caring organization. The records
that parishes make will themselves form important historical
documents and must be of a high standard.

In each parish the churchwardens must keep a terrier of all lands
and an inventory of all articles belonging to the church, together
with a logbook recording all alterations, additions, repairs and
events affecting the church and its property, including the churchyard.[8] The terrier should show any extensions to the churchyard.
The inventory should list monuments of historical interest,
indicating if they are listed in their own right, and trees subject

to tree preservation orders, as well as minor items such as a wheel-barrow or a strimmer bought for work in the churchyard. The logbook should record such matters as a repair to the boundary wall, the felling of a dangerous tree or vandalism to graves and the repairs that were carried out as a result. Repairs of any significance not deemed *de minimis* by the chancellor will require a faculty, the details of which should be recorded as well.

The form of the terrier, logbook and inventory must accord with the current recommendations of the Council for the Care of Churches.[9] The churchwardens are required to update and present these records to the PCC as early as possible in each calendar year with a signed statement that they are accurate,[10] as well as a report on the fabric of the church and all articles belonging to the church, based on inspection during the year. Their report, first to the PCC and then to the annual parish meeting,[11] should include the state of the churchyard, particularly major features such as the boundary wall, paths and trees. The churchwardens' responsibility for records and making their reports is to be carried out in consultation with the incumbent or other minister currently responsible for the parish.[12]

There is an important statutory duty for a detailed 'quinquennial inspection' to be carried out every five years by a qualified person, either an architect or chartered surveyor, approved by the diocese for the individual church building concerned.[13] The Council for the Care of Churches' publication *A Guide to Church Inspection and Repair* recommends that a quinquennial inspection should include churchyard structures and boundary walls. The annual report to the PCC should relate to the latest quinquennial report, summarizing progress in implementing its recommendations. There is a special requirement, whether the churchyard is open or closed, for the quinquennial to include any tree that is subject to a tree preservation order[14] and any ruin that is designated by the Council for British Archaeology and the Royal Commission on the Historical Monuments of England (now English Heritage) as being of outstanding architectural, artistic, historical or archaeological value. For this purpose a ruin must be a building above ground, which could include a derelict chapel or a former parish lock-up.[15] The annual report should mention the condition of any substantial memorial, including a mausoleum especially if it is listed, and any other significant development in the churchyard.

Comprehensive records and plans, both written and photographic, should be kept of each churchyard. In the absence of plans, mistakes can occur as to where a body has been buried or whether a grave has been reserved. (A guide to making a churchyard plan is given in Appendix 1.)

The photographic record for a churchyard should be related to the plan and to the file of forms which is discussed below. The forms relating to burials are in addition to the statutory register of burials[16] and should, ideally, be in two parts. One part should cover burials and the other should cover memorials. The forms may conveniently be made on A4 paper, and kept in a ring binder. Older systems may use index cards. Where a memorial relates to more than one burial, the memorial record form should be duplicated and full cross-references dated and added to each copy. If a memorial is removed, for example to allow for reburying in another part of the churchyard, particular care will be needed to record what became of the memorial. It is helpful to build up as full and accurate a record as possible of earlier burials and memorials, with the help of local historical societies and others interested in the subject. Antiquaries in the eighteenth and nineteenth centuries often copied down inscriptions that are now illegible.

The form for each burial should include an up-to-date record of those who are responsible for particular graves and memorials or have an interest in them. Where a grave is no longer cared for by relatives, and especially if a monument becomes dangerous, it may be necessary to repair the monument and perhaps remove it altogether. It will then be important to be able to contact relatives, to demonstrate to the chancellor that all reasonable steps have been taken to establish contact with the heirs.

Parishes should try to devise new systems for keeping in touch with relatives. The formal responsibility for updating the record with any change of address and any addition or substitution of names lies with the relatives but they are rarely conscious of it. A positive means of keeping in contact may be by encouraging relatives to subscribe to a society of friends of the parish church. Any general changes may then be drawn to their attention by regular newsletters from the parish.

Modern computer systems are particularly useful for devising an arrangement of this sort and could be shared between several parishes, perhaps on a deanery basis. It will be essential, however, for such a system to be devised and maintained by people with appropriate expertise, including knowledge of the relevant law, for instance that concerned with data protection. It would be worth working with local history societies that could supply relevant expertise and also house the records safely.

Maintenance

Regular maintenance of the churchyard is both a fundamental duty and also the only way to prevent future difficulties. Maintenance includes straightforward repairs, the resurfacing or laying out of new paths, and the positioning of noticeboards and seats, including the commissioning of new ones. Stonework in a churchyard, such as monuments, paths and boundary walls, and also other items, whether of brick, wood or iron, will require occasional attention. If repairs are carried out in good time, expense will be saved in the long run. Some features may be of considerable historic interest and, whether or not special secular controls apply, such as listing by the Department of Culture, Media and Sport, it will be important that their repair should be carried out only with the advice of a competent conservator. Help in obtaining such advice may be sought from the parish architect or surveyor, from the secretary of the Diocesan Advisory Committee or from the Council for the Care of Churches. Apart from memorials, special care must be taken of such features as churchyard crosses, sundials, stocks and stone coffins.

Damaged monuments need to be repaired as soon as possible, especially if they may be considered dangerous, but the need for urgent action should not cancel out the need for particular care. The work required may seem straightforward but if done inappropriately can cause considerable damage. Leaning stones may need to be straightened into their original position. Ironwork, such as railings around a vault, is now something of a rarity and a planned programme of painting may be needed to protect it and to prevent it from becoming unsightly. Lettering on a monument should not normally be re-cut, although it may be appropriate to clean and repaint it. Where lettering has been obscured by lichen, it is better to leave it undisturbed since the process of cleaning may damage the stone.

Very minor matters indicated as such in directions issued by the chancellor do not need a faculty.[17] Otherwise, most items of maintenance require a faculty. The archdeacon may grant a faculty for resurfacing paths in the same material and with the same appearance, for repairs to walls, fences, gates and lych-gates where matching materials are used, or for providing or replacing a noticeboard or repainting one in a different colour, providing the proposals are unopposed. The archdeacon may also authorize such minor additions as a garden seat, including a memorial inscription, and a discreet floodlighting system to illuminate the church.[18] In such cases the Diocesan Advisory Committee will be consulted as normal.[19] If there is any opposition or possible controversy, or where the archdeacon's own church is concerned, or if there is an emergency requiring immediate work, the matter will be referred to the chancellor.[20]

A PCC should endeavour to agree on and publish its own policies and arrangements for maintenance. They should be clearly displayed and copies should be made readily available to the public, along with the diocesan regulations for new memorials and inscriptions and any variations for the parish which have been approved by the chancellor. They should include general guidance on such matters as grass cutting and tending graves which can be the subject of heated controversy. Devising a suitable policy may pose a considerable pastoral challenge. For some, the attraction of a churchyard is its natural character, with an abundance of wild flowers among long grass. Others want smooth lawns, constantly cut. In general, an area in current use for burials will need to be cut regularly. In a rural parish it may be acceptable to keep the grass down by letting sheep graze at certain periods and in certain places. This arrangement may be managed in sections by means of a single-strand electric fence forming an enclosure which may be moved when the grass within it has been cropped.[21]

Parts of a churchyard that have been enclosed for a long time but have never been used for burials may be particularly rich in plant life and should be maintained with minimal mowing. If the charm of the churchyard is to be preserved, it may be better to reuse ground elsewhere in the churchyard rather than to use these areas

for burials. The desire of relatives to tend graves by laying flowers
and by mowing the grass around them must be balanced against the
practical problems of the flower containers and of the disposal of
wilted or artificial flowers. Whatever the rules in a particular churchyard, it is important to explain them clearly and so avoid upsetting
the relatives. Relatives should also be consulted before any changes
are made to the churchyard which may affect existing memorials.

Diocesan regulations may require that any flower containers
should be of a hard material and sunk completely in the ground
to allow for mowing. Glass can be dangerous if it is broken.
Remembrance Day poppies and Christmas wreaths may be allowed
for a limited period but no other artificial flowers. An alternative is
to encourage the planting of seasonal bulbs.

It is common practice to level grave mounds as soon as they have
fully settled, probably after six months, so as to assist mowing and
to prevent accidents. Kerb stones are rarely allowed nowadays for
new memorials; kerbs to graves that are no longer tended by
relatives may be removed under a faculty for rearranging the
churchyard, as discussed in the next chapter. Kerbs often form a
frame for gravel or stone chippings, but they cannot prevent the
invasion of weeds which can quickly become unsightly. It may be
preferable to turf the interior of the enclosure.

Litter and other nuisances

Litter can spoil the enjoyment of any public place and it can be
particularly distressing in a churchyard. Depositing litter into or
from any place in the open air to which the public have access
without payment is a criminal offence under the Environmental
Protection Act 1990. Abuse of any land in the open air by the
dumping of large items, such as a car or cooker, is treated as a
more serious offence,[22] though the local authority has a duty to
remove abandoned cars.[23] If a churchyard is in a litter control area
created by a local authority, the incumbent and PCC, as occupiers
of the land, may be put under a duty to ensure that it is, so far
as practicable, kept clear of litter and refuse.[24] Local authority
regulations may also penalize dog owners who do not clean up
after their pets. PCCs may wish in any case to discourage such
unthinking use of churchyards.

A common litter problem in a churchyard is the throwing of confetti at weddings. It is prudent for the incumbent and the PCC to have a definite policy on this and to make sure that it is clearly published. The practice may be forbidden or those organizing a wedding may be required to ensure that confetti is cleaned up or to pay an appropriate fee to cover the expense to the church of doing so. Wedding guests need to be made aware of what is allowed. Confetti thrown on a public road outside the churchyard is the concern of the local highway authority; if the incumbent or PCC fail to guard against this becoming a problem, they may be liable for public nuisance.

Noticeboards and advertisements

The level of sensitive care given to regulating churchyard monuments and ensuring worthy inscriptions on them extends also to noticeboards. These are important pointers not only to factual information about the church and the services held there but also to its place in the local community. They need to be clear and attractive, encouraging people to come to church, not drab and uninformative. A faculty will be required for the erection of a new noticeboard or the replacement or repainting in a different colour of an existing board.[25] Secular restrictions on advertising may mean that permission for noticeboards is also required from the local planning authority.

Trees and planting

The Church's control system covers not only burials, noticeboards and other man-made features but also the trees and planting within a churchyard.[26] The chancellor, after consulting with the Diocesan Advisory Committee, is required to give written guidance for parishes in the diocese on planting, felling, lopping or topping trees,[27] which will apply to closed churchyards that the PCC is responsible for maintaining as well as to those still in use.[28] The PCC's responsibility for a churchyard includes both the care of existing trees and proposals for planting new ones.[29] One recompense is that a PCC can dispose of timber from trees in the churchyard and use the proceeds for maintenance of the church or of the churchyard itself.[30]

The consent of the local planning authority will be needed to cut down or carry out work on any trees that are subject to tree preservation orders[31] or are in a conservation area.[32] Wilfully damaging or destroying a protected tree is a criminal offence,[33] unless the tree is dying or dead or has become dangerous, in which case a suitable replacement must be planted as soon as reasonably possible.[34] Work on a protected tree can be carried out to prevent or lessen a nuisance, as where a tree projects dangerously low over a public footpath or where its roots are undermining a neighbouring building.[35] It may be necessary where a tree is undermining or otherwise damaging a significant monument. Even so, the local planning authority should always be notified, preferably in advance. Trees in conservation areas are protected in the same manner as if they were covered by a tree preservation order, unless notice has been served on the local planning authority and it does not make a preservation order within six weeks.[36]

Advice may be obtained from the local authority planning officers responsible for trees. They may prove very reluctant to authorize felling of any trees subject to a tree preservation order and so should be consulted when new trees are planted, in case there are long-term intentions to fell others. Any replacements should be of the same or another appropriate species. The DAC will be able to guide a parish to a sensible choice. Both parish officers and planning staff may well have changed before the planned time for felling arrives. It is therefore particularly important to keep the plan easily accessible and to make it clear where any related correspondence may be found.

It can happen that several mature trees require felling or are suitable for felling at the same time. People can be attached to trees whether they are protected or not, and distressed if they are felled. With foresight, however, potential opposition can be anticipated by planting suitable replacements well in advance and by felling the old trees selectively.

Insurance

In view of their extensive responsibilities if any accident should occur in a churchyard, it is essential for the incumbent and the PCC to be covered by an adequate insurance policy. This should cover repairs other than those caused by normal wear and tear, including, for instance, the reinstatement of a monument or the replacement of a noticeboard damaged by vandals. Insurance must also be taken out in respect of any liability for injury suffered by church staff, members or visitors on account of harm caused by any church staff or by a contractor working in the churchyard, although the contractor may have his or her own policy which will cover all contingencies and indemnify the church authorities. A contractor who negligently causes an accident will normally be liable to the person injured but the church authorities could still be liable as well.

A typical insurance policy should provide a Public Liability limit of indemnity of not less than £5,000,000. This will provide cover in respect of liability arising through negligence or under the Occupiers' Liability Acts to the public including members of the congregation. Employers' Liability cover should also be arranged to cover any liability which may arise following accidents to paid members of staff and all volunteers including those carrying out work in the churchyard. The Employers' Liability (Compulsory Insurance) Regulations 1998 require a statutory minimum limit of indemnity of £5,000,000, although typically insurance policies will provide a higher limit than this of £10,000,000. Insurance policy conditions require churches to take every reasonable precaution to protect and maintain the property, prevent damage or injury and comply with laws, by-laws or regulations. This would include temporary precautions, such as putting up warning notices and roping off an unstable monument or the area around a tower where a pinnacle has become unsafe.

Finance

Nowadays maintenance is generally carried out by volunteers but repairs are paid for by the parishioners. One exception is the expense incurred on the upkeep of ruins in the churchyard, where the Diocesan Board of Finance is responsible, if it has given written approval for works, to implement recommendations contained in a quinquennial report.[37]

Historically, the profit as well as the burden belonged to incumbents. Fees charged for burials were part of their personal income as was money raised from grazing sheep in the churchyard or the disposal of timber or other produce. Now, these sources of income are normally paid to the Diocesan Board of Finance or the PCC.

Tables of fees are regularly compiled by the Church Commissioners and approved by the General Synod under the Ecclesiastical Fees Measure 1986. These include fees for burials, the erection of monuments and searches in church records.[38] A faculty for a monument or the reservation of a grave space will be more expensive and the chancellor will determine the proportion of the fee to be allocated to the incumbent and/or PCC. In some dioceses, a faculty may only be granted on condition that an appropriate sum be paid to the PCC towards the upkeep of the churchyard.

A wise PCC will maintain a separate churchyard account and seek contributions for it through donations, and through contributions from relatives of persons buried in the churchyard. The account may be constituted as a restricted fund, which may only be used for the churchyard, or as a designated fund, which the PCC may decide to draw on for general church purposes if necessary.[39] A churchyard guild or a group of friends may be set up to provide financial and other practical support and may be registered separately as a charity. It is important to bear in mind, however, that gifts to the church or to a special churchyard fund can only be treated as charitable for tax purposes if they are for the churchyard or the church premises as a whole, rather than for the maintenance of a particular grave.

Local authorities and other public bodies

If a churchyard is formally closed, responsibility for burials in the parish will lie entirely with the secular local burial authority.[40] As will be explained in the next chapter, responsibility for the closed churchyard may also be transferred to a local authority.[41] Indeed, under the Open Spaces Act 1906, a local authority has power to take over entire or partial care, management and control of a burial ground that is still in use for burials.[42] This would not normally be appropriate for a churchyard around a church but could be valuable for a detached churchyard where maintenance is proving a drain on parish resources. In such a case, any assets designated for the churchyard may be transferred to the local authority.[43]

Where a churchyard is still in use, the local authority responsible
for burials in the parish concurrently with the PCC has power to
contribute towards the maintenance of the churchyard.[44] The secular
burial authority will normally be the district council,[45] or in
London the council of the relevant London borough. However,
secular parish councils or, in Wales, community councils may also
act as burial authorities or in urban areas where there is no parish
council, a parish meeting may take up this role.[46]

Local authorities, the Heritage Lottery Fund,[47] English Heritage
or charities may also provide for the repair of special features
in a churchyard, particularly any structure that is independently
listed or scheduled as an ancient monument.[48] This could include
a notable mausoleum or chest tomb or an ancient cross, a
lych-gate or stocks. Local authorities generally have power to
contribute to the maintenance of war memorials that may be sited
in a churchyard and may pay for any additions to commemorate
those involved in later wars.[49] Both the DAC and CCC will be able
to provide up-to-date guidance on sources of grant-aid for particular
categories of monuments that change from year to year. There are
also powers to provide new public amenities such as seats and
shelters abutting a road, clocks or lighting.[50] These amenities may
be provided in a churchyard or in other land surrounding a
church.

In the next chapter various more far-reaching provisions are
discussed for transferring responsibility for the upkeep of churchyards to local authorities. Special considerations apply to urban
churchyards, particularly in the inner city where the expense of
maintenance can be onerous for a small and impoverished
congregation. Even where money is limited, it is prudent for
the church community to maintain control and to look after the
churchyard themselves, assisted, perhaps, by a partnership with the
local authority, supported by central government funds under the
Inner Urban Areas Act 1978. This may involve building walls and
fences, planting and other landscape work and restoring
significant structures and monuments in the churchyard.[51]

chapter 6
The changing churchyard

A churchyard expresses a sense of continuity as a focal point for the local community. It provides a setting for the church building in which the Christian liturgy takes place year by year and thus affirms that the memory of those who worshipped in that place in the past is still respected. Change is unavoidable however and, while it may happen more slowly in a churchyard than in the surrounding neighbourhood, it can prove unsettling.

Both in town and country, churchyards often have little space left and it is important to plan for the future by assessing the trends over the next ten or twenty years and the likely number of new burials to be accommodated. It is wise for a plan to be prepared in consultation with the archdeacon. It should include provision for the interment of cremated remains if that has not already been made. Even where a churchyard is closed for burials, such a scheme may be welcomed by the surrounding community.

It may also be worthwhile for the PCC to arrange for professional advice on the landscape aspects of such a plan from either the inspecting architect if he or she has qualifications or experience in landscape design, or from a landscape designer. The effects on a landscape surrounding a building can all too easily be neglected, even where expensive building work, is being carried out (e.g. for an extension). Normally any landscaping of a churchyard should be restrained, for even minor changes such as laying a path or planting a yew hedge can alter the character of a churchyard greatly. As always, it is essential that a faculty is obtained before any changes are made.

Alterations

Changes to a churchyard may involve resiting memorials or even moving human remains, whether to allow for new burials or to use the churchyard more effectively and attractively as an open space. Changes may also be caused by new building, such as an extension to the church, a church hall, new toilets or a tool shed.

New paths may be laid to improve access, especially for disabled people. A well-designed approach may make the church more inviting, with a ramp in addition to steps and provision for vehicles to come close to the church door. It is now an express provision of planning law that the needs of disabled people should be taken into account in any scheme that needs planning permission.[1] Under the Disability Discrimination Act churches will, with effect from 2004, have to take reasonable steps to remove, alter or provide reasonable means of avoiding physical features that make it impossible or unreasonably difficult for disabled people to participate in their services.[2] Any of these changes will require a faculty.

Consultation with outside bodies

Various public bodies, besides the local authority, will be particularly concerned by any changes to the churchyard that may affect archaeological features or remains above or below ground. These bodies include English Heritage, and the statutory amenity societies (see the leaflet *The National Amenity Societies* from the Council for the Care of Churches, listed in the bibliography on page 143 of this book):

- Society for the Protection of Ancient Buildings (SPAB);
- The Georgian Group;
- The Victorian Society;
- The Twentieth Century Society;
- The Ancient Monuments Society (AMS);
- The Council for British Archaeology (CBA).

Any of these has the right to comment on the grant of a faculty or of planning consent and to request particular conditions.

It is obviously important to avoid any risk of damaging archaeological evidence whether above or below ground even by apparently insignificant works. Even small pieces of information, when added to others, may assist in building up a coherent picture of the past. During minor interventions, any find that may be of archaeological significance, whether carved stone, wood, metal or pottery, should be reported via the Diocesan Advisory Committee secretary to the diocesan archaeological adviser as soon as possible. If a find, perhaps made in the course of digging a grave, indicates more extensive archaeological evidence, it may be necessary for the incumbent to direct that a different space should be used for the burial. In the past, any gold or silver had to be reported to the coroner, as it might be claimed by the Crown as treasure trove, but under the Treasure Act 1996, a much wider range of items may now be claimed by the Crown. However, the Church will be granted exemption for items found on unconsecrated land with the exception of any items that would have been treasure trove under the previous law.[3] Guidance should be sought, if necessary, from the coroner.

Relocation of monuments

Monuments should be moved only when it is necessary and with the necessary faculty, not only because of the expense, resentment and worry that can be provoked but also because their full meaning can only be understood in their original context. A monument remains the property of the executors or heirs of the person commemorated and they should always be contacted, if known, before any application is made. The chancellor may require the heirs to be individually cited, that is formally served with a copy of the petition for the necessary faculty.[4]

When considering the proposal to move a monument, account should be taken of the following factors:

1. Monuments that may seem of little interest today may be considered worth preserving by a later generation and should not be removed without good reason. On the other hand, space may be limited – within one generation four or five burials a year can use a substantial area – and it may be better to relocate some old monuments and so allow for reburying, rather than to close the churchyard. It is generally considered that 50 years should have elapsed after the last burial before the area is used again.
2. Monuments standing against the church or churchyard wall may cause damp to rise within the walls.
3. Monuments that retain railings may become choked with weeds and brambles because it is difficult to maintain the ground within the enclosure.

If it is decided for such practical reasons to petition for moving a monument elsewhere, it is important to try to maintain as much as possible. Where there is a footstone as well as a headstone, the smaller stone should be resited at the back of the headstone, ensuring that inscriptions on each stone remain visible. Where monuments form a group, whether visually or belonging to the same family, the group should be kept intact.

Occasionally, churchyard monuments may merit preservation in the church or church porch or even in a museum but this is only suitable for monuments of especial interest. It is no longer considered acceptable to carry out wholesale clearance and then to place headstones around the churchyard wall or to lay them flat as paths. Where the latter course has been adopted, the inscriptions should always be underneath so that they will be protected. In every case where monuments are removed, their original position and appearance must be recorded and the record of the burial place and the churchyard plan amended to show what has been done with them.

Local authorities; transfer of responsibility

As discussed in the previous chapter, there are various powers under which local authorities may assist with the maintenance of a churchyard that is managed by the PCC, whether it is still in use for burials or not. Under the Open Spaces Act 1906, a local authority may agree to take over partial or entire responsibility for the care, management and control of a burial ground.[5] Local authorities for this purpose include county councils, district councils, London borough councils and parish councils. Provided that the churchyard has not been closed by Order in Council, this power allows burials to continue. Even without a formal closure by Order in Council, a local authority may agree to accept control of a churchyard if it is no longer in use for burials and may lay it out as an open space for public use.

Wherever a local authority takes over control of a churchyard under the Open Spaces Act, it has a duty to manage it for the enjoyment of the public as an open space.[6] This will include appropriate levelling and landscaping and perhaps the provision of facilities such as railings, gates, turf, planting, ornaments, seats and lighting. A faculty will be required for any of these installations. Where the local authority has assumed the management of a churchyard under a voluntary agreement, the agreement will be for a set period of time and can be reviewed when it runs out with updated terms. Before any agreement is made or renewed, advice should be obtained from the diocesan registrar.

Where a churchyard has been formally closed, the PCC remains responsible for keeping it in good order and repairing the boundary walls and fences,[7] unless such responsibility has been transferred to a local authority. The PCC may transfer its responsibilities by giving three months' notice[8] to the parish council or meeting. This, in turn, may shift the responsibility to a district council. Where responsibility for maintaining a churchyard was transferred to a local authority before local government reorganization in 1974, the authority now responsible is the one to which a request for the transfer of responsibility would have been made today.[9] To allow for local authority budgeting, it is normal practice for a PCC to give informal notice of the intention to transfer responsibility twelve months before serving formal notice.

Under any of these provisions, the churchyard remains subject to the faculty jurisdiction. If any alterations are to be made, the local authority will normally be responsible for petitioning for the necessary faculty. In other cases, for example if the incumbent and PCC are applying for an area to be set aside and landscaped for cremated remains, the local authority should be cited and made a party in the proceedings.

Closed churchyards

Where a churchyard is full, that is when all the grave spaces have been used for burials, an Order in Council may be made to close it formally. This will end the general right of burial for parishioners and will normally prevent any further burials of bodies, except in individual spaces that have already been reserved by faculty or where there is room in a double depth grave of a relative. Burial contrary to an Order in Council is a criminal offence. However, where remains later have to be disturbed in a closed churchyard, for example to allow for an extension to a church building, they may be reverently reinterred within that churchyard.[10] The incumbent may wish to authorize the interment of cremated remains in existing graves but faculty approval is necessary, especially if any new memorials are to be erected. If such a faculty has been granted, those who would have had a right of burial in the churchyard had it remained open may have a right to burial of cremated remains.[11] The incumbent will usually be given a discretion to allow the interment of cremated remains in other cases. However, the exact terms of the faculty must be carefully observed.

Application for an Order in Council to close a churchyard is made to the Privy Council, through the Coroners' Section of the Home Office. Officials will advise on the publication of notices and will consult with the local authorities for the area.[12] The Secretary of State may provide that powers are included in an Order allowing further restrictions on the future use of the churchyard in addition to prohibiting body burials.[13] In some cases land may have been added to a churchyard by an adjacent landowner, who retains burial rights in the extension under the Consecration of Churchyards Acts 1867 and 1868. This is explained further below. If a churchyard is later closed by Order in Council, a separate Order is required to extinguish such rights.[14]

Searching for the Order to establish whether a churchyard has been closed may be laborious. Copies should be kept in both the parish and diocesan records. If they cannot be found there or in the local record office, the indices of the annual volumes of Statutory Rules and Orders will need to be searched, unless the Home Office is able to provide the answer.[15]

The criteria on which the Home Office will support an application for an Order in Council include not only the obvious problem that the churchyard is full but also requirements of public health and decency and the need to prevent or reduce a nuisance. The application is unlikely to be successful if only part is full, or if there is still space for burials and the parish merely wishes to be saved the expense of maintenance by transferring responsibility to the local authority. Parishioners considering an application for an Order in Council should bear in mind that this is an irreversible step. There is, under current legislation, no provision for reopening a closed churchyard.

Disposal of churchyard land

Churchyards in England and Wales are normally well protected from development but a faculty may be granted for occasional secular uses, e.g. private rights such as an access route to a nearby building, or public facilities such as the construction of an underground electricity substation. Generally any permanent secular building or engineering works using part of a churchyard will only be authorized where it is required under specific statutory provisions. The most likely example is where part of a churchyard is needed for essential road widening.

Building on any disused burial ground is expressly prohibited under the Disused Burial Grounds Act 1884, whether or not the protection of the faculty jurisdiction applies. There is an exception which permits extensions to a church.[16] However, a chancellor may refuse a faculty even for a church extension if it is likely to cause substantial disruption to human remains.[17] Redundant church land may be disposed of by a scheme under the Pastoral Measure 1983. This overrides the Disused Burial Grounds Act 1884 and frees the land for any sort of development,[18] but only if it has not been used for human burials during the preceding 50 years or no relative or personal representative of anyone buried in the land objects. Even if the 1884 Act is overridden, as outlined below, steps will be taken to protect human remains and memorials.

A parish church with its associated land may be declared redundant and taken out of parish use by a pastoral scheme prepared under the Pastoral Measure 1983.[19] Following a detailed report by the CCC, which includes the churchyard, a proposal will be recommended by the diocesan pastoral committee[20] and put forward by the bishop for drafting by the Church Commissioners.[21] After further consultation, the scheme may be confirmed by an Order in Council.[22]

A pastoral scheme relating to a redundant church may itself provide for the future of the whole redundant site,[23] or a supplementary scheme will provide separately for the churchyard. A pastoral scheme relating to a churchyard independently of the church building may appropriate the whole or any part of a churchyard or a detached church burial ground for any purpose 'without limitation of use'.[24] Such a scheme may be made for a churchyard, either where the church itself has not been declared redundant or where there has been a redundancy scheme for the church but no provision has been made for the associated land.[25] The bishop and the Church Commissioners are required to ensure such provision is made in the scheme as appears to them desirable for the future use and amenities of any associated church building and for preserving access to any grave.[26]

In some cases where a redundant church is of particular historic or archaeological interest or of architectural quality, it may be vested in the Churches Conservation Trust[27] (previously known as the Redundant Churches Fund).[28] The transfer may include the whole or part of the churchyard or other land annexed to the church.[29] If the churchyard has not been formally closed by Order in Council, new burials may be permitted by the Trust but only in special cases, as where the deceased had actively cared for the church during his or her lifetime, or family members had been buried there in the past. Special care will be taken by the Trust to ensure the quality of any new memorials.

Redundant sites are generally retained by the Diocesan Board of Finance[30] or disposed of under a redundancy scheme.[31] A church-yard and other associated land may be kept with the church or disposed of separately.[32] Where a redundant church is vested in the Diocesan Board of Finance, that board may be given responsibility for the care and maintenance of land annexed or belonging to the church, including land that is or has been used for burial.[33]

In these cases, the faculty jurisdiction usually ceases to apply. Unless the land is transferred to the Churches Conservation Trust, any legal effects of consecration will similarly lapse[34] as also will any burial rights, subject to the payment of compensation by the Diocesan Board of Finance.[35]

Removal of human remains and memorials after development or redundancy

Where a churchyard is developed, Section 65 and Schedule 6 of the Pastoral Measure 1983 deal with any human remains or memorials that could be affected. If the Secretary of State is satisfied that a scheme will not involve the disturbance of human remains, after consultation with the bishop and the Commonwealth War Graves Commission, he may waive the normal requirements as to human remains but not as to any memorials.[36]

Normally, notice of any proposal to remove remains or memorials must be published, including details specified in the Schedule, on two successive weeks in a local newspaper and displayed in a conspicuous place where the remains are interred. Notice must also be served on the bishop and the Commonwealth War Graves Commission and on the personal representatives or next of kin of anyone whose remains have been interred there over the previous 25 years.[37] The person removing human remains must comply with any directions given by the Secretary of State.[38] The personal representatives or relatives or, in relevant cases, the Commonwealth War Graves Commission must be given two months to remove the remains and any memorial.[39] If they do not do so, the landowner may move the remains and memorials to any land that the bishop specifies. In the case of memorials, the Diocesan Advisory Committee must be consulted and it may be decided to allow the memorials to remain where they are.

If the bishop does not give directions, the new landowner is free to reinter the remains in any cemetery or burial ground or to cremate them and to re-erect the memorials at the new place of burial or at some other appropriate site.[40] As a last resort, the landowner may offer an unclaimed memorial to the bishop. If, after consulting with the Diocesan Advisory Committee, the bishop does not accept it for preservation, the memorial may be disposed of but must first be broken and defaced.[41] The landowner must deposit with both the local authority and the Registrar General a full record of any memorial that is removed from the land where it was originally sited.[42]

A memorial is protected even if it commemorates someone who is not buried on the land being cleared. Only after any such memorial has been disposed of in accordance with directions from the bishop, or after the bishop has given a dispensation from any special arrangements, in either case after consultation with the Diocesan Advisory Committee, can development proceed. The bishop has the power to impose reasonable conditions for the removal of either remains or memorials, for example the creation of a new memorial or a Book of Remembrance to commemorate people whose remains have been moved.[43]

Extensions to churchyards

Where land is to become used for burials as a churchyard, planning permission will be required for a change of use,[44] but even in rural or green belt areas where change of use would normally be discouraged, a churchyard extension may, nevertheless, be acceptable. Parishes must consult the DACs to discover whether the proposed area is archaeologically sensitive.

There is encouragement according to various Victorian provisions for local landowners to donate land for an extension. If they do so under the Consecration of Churchyards Act 1867 and 1868, they may retain the perpetual right to burial in up to 41.8 sq. m (50 sq. yd) or one sixth of such land.[45] Even if a parish has to buy the land for an extension or a totally new churchyard, they may find in the countryside that the market price is little more than the agricultural value.

Possibilities exist for partnerships with the local authority. A parish may feel that however attractive the local municipal cemetery may be, they would prefer to create or extend a churchyard which has continuity with a worshipping community. An arrangement may be made with a burial authority for land to be provided for a cemetery next to or near an existing churchyard or perhaps adjacent to a new church.

With mutual cooperation, glebe land could be made available for this purpose,[46] especially if it is next to a churchyard. It can be allocated as a churchyard extension by the diocese and consecrated. It may be possible to persuade the local authority to bear the initial expense of laying out and landscaping the site and to remain responsible for maintenance. The consecrated area may be linked with an existing churchyard or church by the use of planting or walls, or separated by similar means from the remainder of a municipal cemetery.[47]

Secular burial authorities have a statutory power to provide burial grounds.[48] District councils or London borough councils may even compulsorily purchase suitable land subject to the approval of the Secretary of State.[49] Under the Places of Worship Acts 1873 and 1882, a local authority, even if it is not a burial authority, has power to provide any number of sites of up to one acre for church use, including sites for burial, again subject to the approval of the Secretary of State.[50] It is also possible for an existing secular burial ground or part of one to be transferred to a church. This must normally be paid for at market value but a lesser payment or none at all may be required if the Secretary of State approves or where the transfer is under a short lease of up to seven years.[51]

Many nineteenth- or twentieth-century churches, especially in towns, have no churchyard but stand in grounds that form their curtilage.[52] Whether or not this is consecrated, it will be subject to the faculty jurisdiction.[53] The bishop may be prepared to consecrate part of such land as an area for cremated remains but this should not be done if the land may later be needed for other purposes, such as a car park or playground.

A secular burial authority may seek consecration of part of a cemetery, provided that it leaves sufficient unconsecrated land for general use.[54] Consecration will bring such an area within the jurisdiction of the chancellor, though, over the years, chancellors have rarely exercised control over consecrated parts of cemeteries which are not attached to a parish church, unless a controversy arises over a cemetery chapel or the movement of remains or the wording of an inscription.[55] Day-to-day control over a cemetery is generally exercised by the local authority staff under their own regulations,[56] although the disposal of a consecrated cemetery chapel is generally considered to require a redundancy procedure under the Pastoral Measure 1983.

chapter 7

The treatment of cremated remains

The effect of cremation on churchyards

Since its introduction in the late nineteenth century, cremation has gradually become the usual form of disposal of bodies in Great Britain. As recently as 1947, cremation was chosen in only 10 per cent of cases but the proportion has increased dramatically until it now accounts for nearly 75 per cent of cases, a percentage that is still gradually rising.

There is another statistic relating to cremations that has gone up significantly. This is the proportion of cases where the remains are taken away from the crematorium by representatives of the dead person, rather than being interred there. This has roughly tripled over the past 25 years, with nearly 45 per cent of remains now being taken away after the cremation. Although we have no firm statistics about what proportion of these are eventually buried in churchyards and church burial grounds, we can deduce that there has been a substantial increase in the demand for burial of cremated remains in churchyards, a deduction confirmed by the experience of many parish priests.

The situation varies in different parts of the country. Interment appears to be more popular in rural areas, especially where there are attractive churchyards with adequate space left for burials and, perhaps, no crematoria in convenient range. On the latter point, however, new crematoria are still being opened and may stimulate a marked change in local practice, when they fill what was previously a large gap.

The common law right of burial enjoyed by parishioners, those on the electoral roll or those who die in the parish, applies to cremated remains as well as to interments. This means that the traditional 'public service' role of Church of England churchyards has now been extended indefinitely. By its very nature cremation allows much greater use of the space available for burials, especially if the methods used to inter and to mark the cremated remains are selected appropriately.

This extension of the public right of burial creates not just a legal obligation, but also a pastoral opportunity. Many mourners, not necessarily with a 'church' or religious background, will appreciate the benefits of a churchyard as a place to come and grieve. This can sometimes afford a means of pastoral contact, through which a person can be made to feel part of the church community.

The need for a policy

Each PCC should have a policy on the burial of cremated remains and should review it from time to time. The policy needs to address:

1. the choice of an area where cremated remains will normally be interred (sites hard against the walls of a church or listed or scheduled features within a churchyard should be avoided);
2. the method of interment, especially with regard to the desirability of biodegradable containers for the ashes;
3. the type of memorial, if any, to be provided;
4. exceptions to be permitted to the general rules.

Of these, the question of a memorial, whether it is to be a tablet in the ground or in a wall, or by an inscription in a Book of Remembrance, will be the hardest to decide.

It may be useful, before discussing practicalities, to attempt two lists of desiderata, one from the PCC's point of view and one from that of the mourners. As might be imagined, these do not entirely coincide.

From the PCC's point of view, the following points need to be considered:

1. Sustainability: The methods for the disposal and for commemoration must be economical in their use of space, and must be capable of being sustained for as long as possible.
2. Practicality: Arrangements must be easy to explain and manage, and must be acceptable to those who look after the churchyard, e.g. in the provision for mourners' flowers.
3. Appearance: Any area allocated for cremated remains must remain in keeping with the rest of the churchyard.
4. Character: Any area provided should be designed to be as pleasant as possible for mourners.

From the mourners' point of view, the only points in the PCC list that will be of direct concern are 2 and 4. Their own concerns will focus more on:

1. An identifiable spot for the burial.
2. A marker with the name of the deceased.
3. A small area to tend and cherish.

These wishes, however understandable, are likely to conflict with almost all of the concerns of any responsible PCC.

Experience has shown that to permit individual memorial markers can create major problems, especially where space is limited and there are likely to be many burials to accommodate. The fundamental difficulty is the concept of an identifiable spot for the interment. This leads to the desire for a memorial at that spot, and the creation of a mini-grave. Many mourners will seek to personalize this. PCC rules may restrict what should be done but in practice it may be pastorally difficult to deal with embellishments which appear, such as a border of chippings round a plaque, a vase, or even miniature plastic fences around the 'plot'. It is not difficult to illustrate these tensions, but much harder to find ways of resolving them.

Much depends on the relationship of the churchyard to the area it serves. Is the parish in a town centre, suburb or rural location? How have cremated remains been dealt with up till now? How many burials are anticipated, and how much space is available?

Where there is a substantial churchyard serving a sparse rural population, it makes little sense to speak of problems of sustainability. If there are unlikely to be more than one or two burials of cremated remains per year, one cannot seriously argue that space will run out. In such cases, there may be little objection to mini-graves with individual markers, if that approach has been agreed by both the PCC and the community at large.

To consider the other extreme, town centre, suburban or even some semi-rural churchyards may have little space and an increasing number of burials to be accommodated. If these obvious difficulties have been pointed out during the initial discussions there may be little difficulty in demonstrating that other solutions must be found. The hardest cases are undoubtedly those where individual markers have hitherto been the norm but where they are becoming unsustainable and so the overall policy must be reviewed.

The area for the interment of cremated remains – 'Garden of Remembrance'

It might be thought that all churchyards will by now include an area for cremated remains, usually referred to as a 'Garden of Remembrance', but a surprising number have not. In some cases, a start may have been made in the past, but either the area has proved insufficient or has been found to be unsatisfactory and a fresh start is needed. Once a parish has decided in principle to set aside an area for cremated remains, the PCC should apply for a faculty with proposals showing not only the extent of the area but how it will be demarcated and landscaped, how interments will be commemorated and what features such as seats, etc. are to be provided.

The aim should always be to create a pleasant area for mourners. If possible, the area should not be directly overlooked by nearby buildings, should benefit from good natural light, and should relate sensibly to existing features of the churchyard such as paths and mature trees. It is sensible to keep the area well away from the church itself to avoid difficulties when maintenance work is to be done on the building. The erection of scaffolding and ladders and the materials associated with such work are bound to be disruptive. Thought should be given to planting, to provision of a seat, some-where to put flowers, and so on. Much can be achieved by good landscaping to develop what can be called 'a sense of place'. If the Diocesan Advisory Committee has a landscape architect member, he or she may be willing to advise on these matters. It is also important to consider how to demarcate the area, whether by concrete edging or low hedges or walls. In the future, everyone will need to be clear as to the extent of the area and depending on the policy of interments, to be able to pinpoint the location of a burial.

Burial of cremated remains outside the designated area

While it is generally wise to set aside a specific area for cremated remains and so avoid a haphazard scattering of such interments, there will be exceptions to the rule. The most obvious case is where cremated remains are placed in an existing family grave already occupied by a body. For example, the children of a deceased couple may wish to bury the cremated remains of one parent in the grave in which the other parent has already been interred. An additional inscription can usually be put on the existing headstone, or else a replacement headstone provided. This can be done at the incumbent's discretion without a faculty. The incumbent may also give permission on occasion for cremated remains to be buried in some other spot. Again, no faculty is required, although it can create a dangerous precedent and lead to difficulties in recording the locations of such burials.

The other question that arises occasionally is the burial of cremated remains within the church building. If the church is consecrated, a faculty is required. A faculty will generally be granted only if the application relates to someone of particular significance in the life of that church, for example a long-serving incumbent. Disposal within the fabric of walls of a church is not regarded as good practice, as by definition it involves disturbance to the structure. Disposal beneath the floor may occasionally be acceptable, providing firm safeguards are met. Heating and lighting ducts must be avoided and both the PCC's architect and an archaeologist should also be consulted in order to satisfy the Diocesan Advisory Committee that no damage will be done. Any inscription can be incised directly on an existing flagstone, or else a sympathetic memorial can be erected either over the spot or on an adjoining wall. A high standard of design and lettering should be sought.

Methods of interment

The use of caskets for the burial of cremated remains is not recommended because it impedes the natural processes of decay and absorption within the ground. But, without a casket, what is the best process of interment? The Christian tradition for decently interring the remains of the departed has always been burial. 'Scattering' can be unseemly and distressing to the bereaved as the remains can be visible for some time, and should normally be avoided. One recommendation is to form a hole between 450 mm (18 in) and 600 mm (2 ft) deep by means of a 150 mm (6 in) auger or boring tool. The cremated remains will arrive in some kind of container from the crematorium and can be gently poured into the hole and then immediately, to avoid upsetting the bereaved, a thin layer of earth sprinkled over the top. If there is a wish to have several interments in the same hole, then a stout oak board should be placed over the layer of earth, and the remainder of the hole filled in on top of the board, as soon as the service of committal has been concluded, and then turfed over. The point of the stout wooden board is that it avoids the possibility of disturbance; and it also means that when the next interment takes place, the topsoil can be removed down to the board, the board lifted up, and the whole process repeated. No ashes should be interred less than 100 mm (4 in) below the surface of the soil. Clearly circumstances will vary from place to place, but this method is strongly recommended as being both seemly and economical in its use of space.

Although direct committal into the earth is, from the point of view of both symbolism and sound practical sense, the wisest course to be followed in all cases, many parishes have still to recognize the drawbacks of interring caskets, especially those made of hardwood or some form of plastic. Even biodegradable caskets will slow the process of dispersal of the remains and therefore will lengthen the period of time before the ground can be used for further burials. For these reasons containers, of whatever kind, should be dispensed with after the actual moment of interment. There are a number of ways in which this can be done, for example the base of the casket provided by the undertaker may be removable, allowing the priest or undertaker to kneel by the hole and pour in the remains.

Exhumation

Requests are occasionally received by registrars for permission to move cremated remains, for a variety of reasons but often because a surviving spouse is intending to move to another part of the country. It is a matter for chancellors to decide whether the request should be granted; on the whole they are reluctant to approve such applications. One argument for the use of a durable form of casket is that it makes it easier to recover the remains should this ever be required. This is unlikely to be accepted as a valid argument in their favour.

Individual memorials

The question of individual markers was touched on earlier. The single most common method of commemoration for cremated remains has become the placing of individual flush markers of stone or slate directly above the burial. In most cases the maximum size is 450 mm x 300 mm (18 in x 12 in), which is in fact quite a substantial stone for the purpose, but the size can be considerably less, such as 300 mm x 230 mm (12 in x 9 in) or even smaller.

Individual markers of this type can give rise to some difficult problems:

1. Over time, they take up and effectively sterilize a lot of space.
2. They offer insufficient space for more than names and dates, and thus form inadequate memorials.
3. They do not age well and have a tendency to settle at an angle.
4. They add to the difficulties of churchyard maintenance; in particular, when they are hidden by surrounding grass, damage can be caused by or to the mower.
5. If neatly laid out and well maintained, they can look regimented; if not, they can look messy.

fig. 1
Neatly laid out individual markers can look regimented.

© Jonathan MacKechnie-Jarvis

fig. 2
Untidy
individual
markers for
cremated
remains.

© Jonathan
MacKechnie-Jarvis

6. There are sadly few examples of flush plaques that have been designed and lettered with some individuality and imagination and most are machine-lettered products.
A recent fashion for standard-pattern cast bronze plaques fixed on to plain stone slabs is generally even more out of keeping with the standards of lettering expected in churchyards.

fig. 3
Machine
lettered
memorials.

© Jonathan
MacKechnie-Jarvis

fig. 4
Miniature
headstones
used to
mark
cremated
remains.

© Jonathan
MacKechnie-Jarvis

Flush plaques are not the only type of memorial stone used for cremated remains. In some rural churchyards headstones are used, indistinguishable in size and style from those used to mark burials of bodies. This obviously gives more scope for a satisfying memorial, but there is an incongruity in using a marker that is so large in relation to the remains themselves. It is also extravagant in its usage of space and is frankly at odds with the whole concept of

fig. 5
The worst
type of
solution – a
jumble of
different
types of
memorial.

© Mary Bliss

cremation. Miniature headstones can also prove to be unsatisfactory, because of the 'pet's cemetery' impression that is created when used *en masse*. In some churchyards the policy seems to be to allow any form of marker provided that it is not too large. The result is a jumble of small headstones, vases, flush or angled plaques, open books, cherubs and hearts.

Alternatives to individual memorials

There is no one solution to these problems which can be applied universally. In many churchyards the use of individual stone plaques is rapidly becoming an embarrassment and yet there is a strong pastoral desire for some form of personal commemoration. The main question is whether this should be on a communal basis, i.e. with a number of names recorded on one memorial or by the use of individual markers of a different sort. Three case studies from Gloucestershire may be of interest.

St George's, Cam is a church serving a semi-rural/suburban parish with a population of 4,000. Here, the practice for some years had been to allow individual cast brass plaques of standard size to be fitted in a continuous row on a stone kerb along one of the paths to the south-east of the church tower. People accepted that there was thus no direct link between the spot of burial and the marker.

fig. 6
Cam,
St George –
memorials
on brass
plaques
along a
stone kerb.

© Jonathan
MacKechnie-Jarvis

65

Predictably, space on the kerb became exhausted, and the PCC decided to create a new Garden of Remembrance. Fortunately the parish possessed a large churchyard extension about 69 m (75 yd) from the church, waiting to be brought into use, part of which was set aside and laid out with herb beds and paths. The paths were given new stone kerbs, on which two rows of brass plates could be accommodated. Much thought was given to landscaping. The result can be regarded as reasonably satisfactory, and should be sustainable for many years to come.

It is worth noting that, in the process of discussing this project, the Diocesan Advisory Committee had urged that individual markers should be abandoned but the PCC argued strongly that it would be pastorally difficult to enforce such a change when so much space was available within the extension churchyard.

fig. 7
Cam,
St George – the
new Garden of
Remembrance.

© Jonathan MacKechnie-
Jarvis

St Mary's, Wotton under Edge serves a market town with a population of 5,500. In this case, the use of individual stone flush plaques over some 20 years had taken up the bulk of the space that had been set aside for a Garden of Remembrance. Sufficient space remained for burials, but only if some new place for recording names could be found. The adjoining churchyard wall contained a blocked doorway and it was decided to fill this with a substantial communal memorial on which names would be carved periodically. This marker is likely to serve for about 20 years, not an extensive period, but much longer than would have been possible by continuing with individual stone plaques.

fig. 8
Wotton under Edge, St Mary – names carved onto a slab in a blocked doorway.

© Jonathan MacKechnie-Jarvis

The work was designed and installed by Rory Young from Cirencester (though subsequent names have been entrusted to another letter-cutter, who has not been able to match the preceding work exactly, thus compromising the harmony of the composition). To make best use of space, the names are inscribed continuously from left to right and so on down; one Christian name only and surname are permitted, with decorative flourishes between each person's name, and at the end of each year. Individual dates of birth and death are not given. At the top is inscribed the text 'I am the Resurrection and the Life'.

A simpler approach to communal markers can be found at Upton
St Leonards, which is a semi-rural village with a population of
1,600. Here oblong stone markers of about 300 mm x 1200 mm
(12 in x 48 in) are used alongside a path, and names are cut
cumulatively under the simple heading 'Here lie the ashes of'.
In this case, names are listed in columns, centre-justified within
dividing margins, and without individual dates of birth and death.
The remains are buried nearby, without containers. The result is
unpretentious but it has proved acceptable pastorally, and avoids
the disadvantages of individual plaques.

fig. 9
Upton
St Leonards –
rectangular
communal
stone markers
alongside a
path.

© Jonathan
MacKechnie–Jarvis

With imagination and sufficient funds to pay both for an appropriate
design and for material of high quality, a wide range of communal
markers can be conceived. They can incorporate sculpture or
lettering to act as a focus for reflection, for which a high standard
of design and execution should always be sought. The cost of such
a marker can be recovered over time within the parochial fees
structure. It is not of course compulsory for mourners to add the
deceased person's name to the memorial, but if it is to be done, it
should be on terms laid down by the PCC, to which no exception
should be made. It has already been noted how the effect of good
design can be marred if future inscriptions are not of the same
standard.

fig. 10
Communal
memorial at
North
Mymms.

© Jonathan Goodchild

Time-limited memorials

A possible answer to the difficulties of proliferating individual memorials is to establish a system of time limits whereby a memorial is authorized for a fixed period of years only. Such a system allows for an element of recycling after the initial and entirely appropriate emotional need for commemoration has passed. After the period of time specified had passed, the memorial would be removed, unless permission were renewed, but with due respect and especial care not to disturb any remains beneath.

Use of walls for memorials

In a number of churchyards, memorials for cremated remains have been incorporated into walls. In some cases, a purpose-built wall has been created: more commonly the churchyard wall is used but this practice can be problematic if the wall itself is of historic interest. With care, marker stones can be accommodated into the face of a wall, and the gradual effect of weathering and lichens will produce a pleasing, organic effect. An attempt at this can be found at Patterdale (Cumbria). In practice the effect is easily spoiled by insensitive additions. This can be seen at Clovelly (Devon), where the idea started well with a fine memorial, which was illustrated

fig. 11
Stone markers placed on the churchyard wall at Patterdale.

© Jonathan MacKechnie-Jarvis

in the second edition of *The Churchyards Handbook*. Subsequent additions included small rectangular blocks of polished granite, projecting from the face of the wall and disturbing the varied and restrained effect that was presumably the original intention.

The other problem of wall memorials is sustainability. Space on most walls will inevitably be limited and a rather curious appearance will be created if large areas of wall are successively filled to capacity with small memorials. If a time limit approach is adopted (see above), it may be difficult to extract earlier memorials. Certainly the weathering process will have to start again.

Books of Remembrance and other means of communication

An alternative to individual or communal markers is the Book of Remembrance, normally kept in the church. These can be obtained, together with the necessary container and stand, from commercial suppliers but it is preferable to commission the pieces for the specific setting in which they will be placed. So far as the book itself is concerned, there are many calligraphers and book-binders who can produce fine work at reasonable cost. The point has often been made before that the best is not necessarily the most expensive – particularly as local craftspeople are quite often below the VAT threshold.

In the Book of Remembrance can be inscribed the names of all those whose ashes have been interred in the churchyard, the cost of the calligrapher's work being added to the fee charged for the interment. The names can either be inscribed chronologically or on a separate page for each date of the year, with the book being opened every day at the appropriate page. A place should be provided where people can put flowers on the anniversary of the funeral, or possibly a candle-stand might be provided nearby. There are various systems that can be operated. Many churches have both a book and a system of individual or communal markers. All interments are recorded in the book, with the inscription on a marker being optional. It is important to note however that a Book of Remembrance is not the same as a record of burials, which needs to be kept in all cases.

If a Book of Remembrance is to be the main form of memorial, it will normally be appropriate to have some form of inscription at the actual Garden of Remembrance. It is surprising how often a pastoral opportunity is missed here. Many such inscriptions will say no more than 'Garden of Remembrance' or 'This Garden of Remembrance was opened on . . .'. How much better to choose an appropriate text from Scripture such as: 'The souls of the righteous are in the hand of God.' In Gardens of Remembrance where individual markers are not allowed, a well-lettered text of this sort may be a welcome focus for grief.

Alternatively, families of the deceased may welcome a more practical and tangible commemoration, such as paying for particular repairs and improvements, or the conservation of important furnishings, such as organs, bells or Royal Arms. A modest inscription may be acceptable but the question must be raised from the beginning with the DAC.

chapter 8

Commissioning a memorial

How do you organize a memorial for someone who has died?
Few people confronted with that task will have any real idea where
to start, and it is important that all concerned in the operation of
churchyards keep this firmly in mind. The procedures governing
memorials and the restrictions on what is permissible can easily
seem complex and heavy-handed to those recently bereaved.
Disagreements can rapidly become major issues to members of
the family and can cause serious pastoral difficulty.

Memorials from catalogues

Much has been written about the depressing standard of churchyard memorials. There is however a good deal of confusion about
the issues involved, which it is the purpose of this chapter to clarify.

Most churchyard memorials are mass-produced ready-shaped
stones which are lettered to order. For many years, the most
common method of applying lettering has been by pantograph-
controlled engraving machine, but more and more use will be
made in the future of computer techniques, which give a far wider
range of design possibilities. Many monumental masons use these
methods and now do no hand-cut lettering of the traditional type.
Their job comprises taking an order, either directly with the client
or from a funeral director, setting up and processing the desired
lettering and finish on a blank memorial, and fixing it at the
churchyard. Designs are selected from a catalogue, with any
innovations being derived from the development of new styles by
wholesalers. The monumental mason will normally have a good
knowledge of what is permitted in churchyards, and the net result
is a high degree of uniformity of shape, material, finish and lettering.

Memorials of individual character

Mourners will on occasion want to commission a more individual
memorial and it is important that advice is available to them so that
this opportunity is not lost. In most areas of the country there are
independent designers/craftspeople who can be commissioned to

fig. 12
Memorial
carved by a
good-quality
high street
mason.

© Jonathan
MacKechnie-Jarvis

produce memorials on an individual basis. A design can be prepared to suit the wishes of the people involved – material, dimensions, shape, lettering and decoration being capable of almost infinite variation, subject only to the churchyard regulations.

It is misleading however to make a blanket distinction between 'high street trade masons' on the one hand, and independent designers/craftspeople on the other. There are many within the memorial industry who wish to promote genuine individuality, and there are certainly some monumental masons who can provide hand-cut lettering and decoration to suit their clients' wishes. It is well worth the extra time and trouble to visit at least two different firms.

Given the rapid development of computer-driven technology, one should also be cautious about regarding as inferior all work that is not cut by hand. It is true that pantograph-controlled machine-cut lettering tends to be dull in character. This is because of the restricted range of typefaces and font sizes available and because of the technical constraints, which, for example, make it hard to achieve sharply cut and elegant serifs to the letters, and impossible to do anything that is not on a straight line. However, computer-controlled laser cutting or sandblasting will eventually give almost infinite scope for lettering and decoration of stone and, especially if hand-finished, the results may be very good.

There are two important limitations to the potential of such technology, which will mean that the finest work will always be by designer/craftspeople, working with traditional skills. First, the result can only be as good as the quality of the design and layout. Nearly all the best letter cutters are trained designers who have worked in a broad range of media. In other words, designing headstones is only part of their experience, and this will show in the quality of their work. Design of a memorial may seem to an outsider to be a simple matter, but for the best results, experience and design flair come together to produce a balanced layout with sensitive use of space, letter forms, decorative detail and so on.

Secondly, lettering by hand allows complete freedom from the constraints of any technology. The skill of the letter cutter lies in knowing when and where to break from absolute regularity. All sorts of adjustments to depth, spacing, size of letters can be made, and the result is a subtle harmony that at present is impossible to replicate by mechanical means.

Choice of stone

There is a wide range of British stones that are suitable for memorial work. These include limestones, sandstones, slates and granites, of many different textures and colouring. In some cases supplies are plentiful and consistent in quality. Some monumental masons will prefer to restrict themselves to these sources. However, there are other stones that are eminently suitable, but where the supply situation is more difficult. The client will have to be prepared to wait for stone of suitable quality to become available, and the mason will have to select the stone carefully at the quarry.

Most stones will change in appearance as they weather. This is a natural process, as is the growth of mould and lichen, which enhances their appearance. British stones, other than slate or granite, will usually weather down to a greyish tone. An exception is Blue Hornton, which oxidizes to an earth-brown colour.

The following lists of stones have been prepared in consultation with geologists, monumental masons and architects. They make no claim to be exhaustive and are intended to be used only as a guide.

British limestones

Portland (Dorset), Purbeck (Dorset), Chicksgrove (Dorset), Blue Hornton (Oxfordshire), Limpley Stoke (Wiltshire), Hopton Wood (Derbyshire).

British sandstones

Grinshill (Shropshire), Kerridge (Cheshire), Woodkirk, Ringby, Bolton Woods, Crosland Hill (Yorkshire), Clashach (Elgin, Scotland).

British slates

Cornwall, Wales, Cumbria.

British granite

Other stones

Stones from outside a particular region may be acceptable as substitutes for indigenous stones that had previously been used in the diocese or parish but are no longer available in sufficient size or quality. The main criterion in this instance is that the stone is in harmony with its surroundings, rather than its country of origin. Some stones have long traditional links with England, such as Caen stone from Normandy or Tournai marble from Belgium. Recently, the beautiful and durable limestones of Northern Italy and some of the French limestones have been chosen for use in cathedral restorations, for instance at Canterbury, and certain Portuguese stones may also be worthy of consideration. Granite from Italy and France and other imported granites are consistent in quality and readily available. If there are reservations over the inclusion of any particular type on a list of stones acceptable in the diocese, a sample should always be requested from the local masons.

When erecting stone memorials in the environs of a stone-built church of historic and architectural distinction, it is desirable to remain consistent with that character. Local stone may not be currently of a suitable quality, but whatever is chosen should be of a similar shade and texture to the materials of the church. In an urban area where the church is not built of stone, or in a church-yard extension where the burial ground is well screened from the church, there may be instances where a greater variety of stone is not out of place, and indeed may add interest to an otherwise dull area. As is said elsewhere in this handbook, the question of context is all-important in deciding what material to use in a particular sit-uation.

The commissioning process

Most churchyard regulations stipulate a minimum period that must elapse before a memorial is erected. There are good practical reasons for this, as at least six months is usually needed to allow the soil to settle, and any attempt to erect a headstone prematurely may involve later work to correct problems caused by soil movement. A reasonable lapse of time also allows mourners to consider different types of memorial, and to select suitable wording for the inscription.

For these reasons it is regrettable when orders for memorials are taken by the funeral director very soon after the death. It is under-standable that mourners today are attracted by the idea of a total 'package' that takes care of every aspect of a death. They may also have a desire to get over the sad business quickly so that they can carry on with their lives. However, decisions can easily be confused by conflicting emotions, and mourners would be better advised to allow time to go by before they consider the question of a memorial.

It is noticeable that where the death has been tragic or premature, not only is there a greater desire to commission a memorial but there is a greater appreciation of the need to obtain a design of real quality. In such circumstances especially, a Diocesan Advisory Committee secretary should be able to provide parish clergy and others with a list of suitable designers/craftspeople and monumental masons with the appropriate skills.

People, particularly those still traumatized by a recent bereavement, may find it difficult to enter into the process of commissioning an individual memorial, rather than take the easier path of choosing something from a catalogue in a monumental mason's showroom.

There are several reasons for this:

- Most independent designers/craftspeople do not advertise, and the mourner may not know of their existence.
- Most independent makers work from home and can only be contacted by appointment. This in itself is off-putting to some, and more 'difficult' than walking into a retail premises.
- The process of design and making is likely to take longer from an independent maker, and the mourner may already be suffering a sense of guilt at the passage of time.
- There may be a concern that anything one-off will run into problems with churchyard regulations and may contrast uncomfortably with other conventional memorials in the churchyard.

Most people experienced in handling enquiries for churchyard memorials will deal sensitively with the person concerned, and will be able to give reassurance on the last two points, and indeed may be able to offer much sympathetic guidance in translating the

fig. 13
Memorial
designed and
carved by
Bettina
Furnee for
Memorials by
Artists.

© Oliver Riviere

person's ideas into a suitable design. Thus can begin a genuinely therapeutic process, very different from the quick decision from a showroom catalogue.

The person seeking a special memorial will certainly need tenacity and patience, and will benefit from encouragement and a helping hand. It may be helpful if he or she is put in touch with 'Memorials by Artists', a specialist agency (now a charity) founded in the late 1980s by Harriet Frazer, who had faced the dilemma of wanting something purpose-made to commemorate her young stepdaughter, but not knowing how to start. 'Memorials by Artists' can put a mourner in touch with a suitable letter cutter, and then advise on the whole process of commissioning, thus taking much of the anxiety out of the process. A modest fee is charged for this service but clients have the satisfaction of being sensitively guided to a solution appropriate to their own circumstances.

fig. 14
A simple and elegant head-stone by James Salisbury.

© James Salisbury

Specially designed and handmade memorials are not necessarily much more expensive than the standard mass-produced examples for several reasons.

- Many independent makers are not registered for VAT, because of their limited turnover. This offers an immediate saving to a private purchaser.
- The independent maker usually has lower overheads: for example he or she may work from home, and have no retail premises or support staff costs to meet.
- The raw materials for a headstone are relatively cheap. Stone purchased direct from a UK quarry will not incur the intermediaries' costs associated with imported blanks such as are used by the monumental industry.

Experience also shows that, for many mourners, cost is in any case a secondary aspect. Many people see the erection of the memorial as a last opportunity to do something for the person who has died. The important thing is to get the memorial right. For any type of memorial, machine-processed or handmade, there is a range of choices between complicated and plain designs. A designer/craftsperson can prepare something of real quality but simple in scope, which can be priced modestly.

Regulations for memorials

The relationship between churchyard regulations and the memorials that appear in churchyards has already been mentioned in this chapter. It can be argued that the repetitive nature of modern churchyard memorials is a result of too much restriction in what is allowed. This argument can be challenged by reference to the many well-designed memorials that fall within the terms of what is normally allowed. However, while churchyard regulations can exclude what is seen as undesirable or unreasonable, they cannot of themselves ensure the creation of good designs.

Independent letter cutters have reported difficulty in getting their designs accepted by parish clergy for three main reasons.

1. Some clergy are wary of designs that are at all out of the ordinary, and advise the person commissioning the memorial that a faculty will be required, when in fact the memorial does fall within the standard provisions that the clergy are allowed to

authorize locally. For example, simple embellishment depicting religious or occupational symbolism may be deemed to need a faculty, since the relevant churchyard rules require faculties for statuary, whereas the rule is intended to apply only to three-dimensional carving.

2. Regrettably some clergy seem to resent spending time dealing with memorial applications, regarding it as a distraction from their 'real' work. The more out-of-the-ordinary the application, the more likely they are to display this attitude. Perhaps more could be done to encourage the view that a memorial is an important part of the grieving process, and is a pastoral opportunity, even if the people concerned are not members of the local congregation.

3. There are specific restrictions within some diocesan churchyard rules stipulating minimum sizes, e.g. for a width of 480 mm (19 in) for memorials. These were introduced following advice in earlier years, not least in earlier editions of this handbook, to curb what were seen as the excesses of many memorials of the late nineteenth and early twentieth centuries. Nowadays this advice may no longer be appropriate as it may rule out – other than by faculty – a well-designed slender memorial. It will produce better results in the long term if those responsible for churchyards are encouraged to welcome creative and individual designs and to focus the churchyard regulations on excluding that which would be genuinely out of keeping, for instance by inappropriate materials or size. Precise dimensions can be left to the good sense of the designer, always bearing in mind that the parish priest can refer for faculty decision anything about which he or she is genuinely unhappy. In doubtful cases, the parish priest would be advised to seek advice from the Archdeacon or Diocesan Advisory Committee secretary, who may well be able to give an encouraging or warning word.

fig. 15
Two examples of
grave markers
enhanced by the
restrained use
of symbolism
related to the
deceased.

chapter 9
The archaeology of the churchyard

The popular conception of a churchyard is of an attractive, perhaps slightly overgrown, garden surrounding an ancient church and filled with graves and gravestones. For most people its chief purpose is as a place of calm and recreation even if they acknowledge its traditional function of providing an area for burials. However, churchyards often have a complex history which may have included a variety of other functions and which in some cases relates back to the origins of Christianity on the site, or even to a pre-Christian use. The surviving traces of this activity make up the archaeology of the churchyard, which, taken all in all, forms an important part of the heritage of the church and of the nation, especially as development erodes so many sites both in town and country.

fig. 16
The ancient churchyard at Elkstone.

© Christopher Dalton

This evidence is fragile; once it has been removed, it is lost for ever. If the archaeology of a church or its churchyard has to be disturbed to allow necessary works, it must be recorded in full to add to our information about the past. The more completely we understand the history and archaeology of a church, its churchyard and the surrounding environment, the greater our appreciation becomes of why a particular place is unique. On a more everyday level, understanding the history of a church also helps a parish to recognize when proposed works of maintenance or development may have archaeological implications.

The history and functions of churchyards

Research is still in progress to establish just how old our earliest churchyards actually are. It is clear that in most medieval parishes, churchyards were in existence by the eleventh century, and of these the majority are likely to be older. The evidence for these dates comes from a variety of sources including the study of the topography of the area and historical documents, and direct evidence such as human remains, grave-markers and finds from archaeological excavations which can now be investigated by sophisticated dating techniques.

Churchyards were not always the tranquil places they generally are today. In the medieval period, some were used for commercial activities. Markets and fairs held within a village or town often occupied the open area around the church and left traces which sometimes survive in the form of pottery and other goods. For example, until 1223 there were apparently skin and cloth markets in the churchyards of St Peter and St Michael, Lincoln. Activities such as bell-casting were frequently undertaken in the churchyard prior to the days of effective transport, and traces of construction activity such as pits for the mixing of mortar or for slaking lime frequently occur near the church.

There may be traces of earlier buildings within the churchyard. The present church may not be the first on the site and may not be directly related to earlier buildings which could lie elsewhere within the enclosure; for example the remains of a Roman villa at Rivenhall in Essex. Foundations, floors or graves may survive from an earlier building or an earlier stage of the existing church.

Immediately adjacent to the present external walls will almost certainly be fragile evidence below the turf that relates to the construction of the building and to any lost portions such as aisles, chapels or porches; evidence that is particularly at risk from well-intentioned attempts to improve the drainage. There may also have been free-standing towers and ancillary buildings. Sometimes, as at Asheldham in Essex, the priest had a house within the churchyard; in urban centres there may be the remains of several houses which at one time encroached on the churchyard.

Some early churches, though the claim can be overstated, may have been deliberately built on top of pagan religious sites. Perhaps more commonly they have been built on land previously settled in the pre-Christian period of which archaeological layers and features may survive. Churchyards can indeed represent 'reservoirs' of archaeological information in a landscape otherwise devoid of archaeological material owing to modern development and re-development. It may be, therefore, that a churchyard contains the only remaining physical evidence of the history of a parish. Even newly-founded Victorian town churches may have post-medieval, medieval or earlier settlement remains surviving in their church-yards, perhaps just under the grass or tarmac surface.

Traces of earlier buildings or occupation, construction activity, and commercial trading are not the only type of archaeological evidence to be found. A churchyard was often used as a dumping ground for items ejected from the church during various periods of its history, for example items deemed superstitious by the six-teenth- or seventeenth-century iconoclasts, or superfluous by Victorian restorers such as fonts, fragments of architecture or sculpture, window glass, tiles, and even machinery such as clocks. These items were either deliberately buried or became covered by vegetation and soil and so eventually forgotten.

During the twentieth century some churchyards, especially in urban locations, were landscaped to provide quiet areas with the idea of creating a space for informal recreation; pathways, seats and schemes of planting were introduced, and these have become a part of the history of the church. The primary function of churchyards was, however, burial and this will be reflected by the presence of a large number of graves, many more than are represented by surviving headstones. Graves have often been disturbed or cut by later burials, especially the medieval ones, which were sometimes quite shallow. It is important to realize that human remains can occur within a few centimetres of the modern land surface so even minor ground disturbance may produce an abundance of bone. Deeper excavation, either for grave digging or more extensive work, may produce grave covers and even entire coffins.

The archaeological planning process

Looking after the archaeology of the churchyard is not an onerous task, provided that a few simple rules are understood and followed. Guidance can always be sought from the Diocesan Advisory Committee.

In recent years there have been various changes to the legal status of archaeology as expressed within the framework of secular planning processes, particularly Planning Policy Guidance Notes (PPG) 15 (1994) and 16 (1990). The need to take account of archaeology has formed part of the requirements of the faculty jurisdiction (the ecclesiastical planning system) for many years but it has been emphasized by the principles introduced by the Planning Policy Guidance Notes so parishes must be made aware of the need to take archaeology into account as part of their stewardship of buildings and churchyards. One of the key messages of PPG 16 and of recent Council for the Care of Churches and Diocesan Advisory Committee guidelines is to urge parishes to consider archaeology at an early stage in any planned works. This is as true of works to a churchyard as it is to work to a church building.

The concept of 'developer pays' in relation to every kind of archaeological intervention was also introduced by PPG 16. In church terms this means that the costs of any archaeological work required prior to programmes of maintenance or development in a church or churchyard are borne by the parish. If the archaeological impact of a scheme is evaluated at an early stage, it is more likely that any associated costs can be minimized through careful planning. Any significant works on a churchyard, as in a church, will require a faculty from the chancellor before they can go ahead. If the planned works will affect the appearance or character of the church or its churchyard, they will also require local authority planning permission.

The Diocesan Archaeological Adviser

When disturbance is planned to the ground of a churchyard, or other works that may have an archaeological impact are to take place (other than routine grave digging and shallow planting), it is wise to inform the Diocesan Archaeological Adviser at an early stage through the normal process of Diocesan Advisory Committee consultation. Works in a churchyard which may have archaeological implications include:

- building an extension to the church;
- erecting a free-standing building;
- digging drains;
- laying cables or pipes;
- installing floodlighting;
- the creation of a new area for cremated remains;
- repair or conservation work to monuments;
- laying new paths or repairing existing ones;
- repairing the churchyard wall or building a new wall;
- repairing a lych gate;
- planting trees.

The earlier such consultation takes place, the less chance there is of unforeseen problems or costs. Even when archaeological deposits exist directly under areas where alterations are planned, a 'mitigation strategy' devised with the help of the Diocesan Archaeological Adviser and Diocesan Advisory Committee will minimize difficulties or may indeed avoid them altogether. If archaeological intervention is unavoidable, it will be necessary to commission a brief. A brief places the required archaeological work within the context of the overall project, outlines what will be required and sets out the research aims and objectives. It will normally be written by the Diocesan Archaeological Adviser or another person approved by him or her.

It is worth noting that contrary to popular belief, archaeologists are not always anxious to dig up your churchyard; in fact the opposite is often true. They prefer to leave archaeological deposits undisturbed and intact if there is no perceived threat, and indeed 'preservation *in situ*' of archaeological deposits is the declared policy of the government. From the Church's point of view, human remains should be left *in situ* wherever possible for both theological and practical reasons, and out of respect for the dead.

Archaeological appraisal

The following paragraphs outline the usual processes carried out to mitigate the archaeological impact of planned works to a church or its churchyard.

The Diocesan Archaeological Adviser will be able to judge the likely impact of disturbances to any significant buried deposits through a process termed 'appraisal'. The likely impact is dependent upon a number of factors. These include the area and depth of the antici-pated excavation, its position in the churchyard and relationship with any standing buildings and the known history of the area, including previous finds, documentary references, and clues in the fabric of the church itself. Once the appraisal is complete, the Diocesan Archaeological Adviser will make a recommendation as to the archaeological implications of the proposed work. There may be no need for any further archaeological involvement; if there is, there are several categories of archaeological recording which may need to be carried out before and/or during the proposed work.

Desk-based assessment

The next step from an appraisal is a thorough desk-based review of all existing archaeological information relating to the area under consideration. As the term implies, this is essentially a documentary exercise, with any fieldwork limited to non-intrusive investigation. No holes will be dug. The information gained at this stage may be adequate, but if not it will be necessary to proceed to the next stage of investigation.

Watching briefs

For minor disturbances, e.g. a trench for a new pipe, or for cables for floodlighting, the recommended course of action is usually precautionary monitoring, often referred to as a 'watching brief'. This simply means having an archaeologist on site during digging operations to double-check that no significant historic deposits are being disturbed. This procedure is often appropriate for other types of disturbance, even as substantial as a small building extension, where this is being constructed on a 'raft' to avoid deep digging. Watching briefs may sometimes, but by no means always, be provided at a modest, even nil cost by local authority personnel or the Diocesan Archaeological Adviser. In some circumstances it may be appropriate for an experienced amateur archaeologist to undertake this responsibility, but only with the prior approval of the Diocesan Advisory Committee. A watching brief is unlikely to be the best response to larger works, which may require an archaeological evaluation or excavation.

Archaeological evaluation

This usually takes the form of a small trial excavation to test the nature of the historic deposits, or a non-destructive survey using geophysics, for example by passing a small electric current underground to determine if walls, foundations or ditches are present, or a combination of these methods. The Diocesan Archaeological Adviser will advise on suitable archaeological contractors who can carry out this work, providing if possible a choice of recommended individuals or organizations who, on invitation by the parish, may then tender for the work as set out in a brief (usually prepared by the Diocesan Archaeological Adviser).

Archaeological excavation

Occasionally, because of the evident importance of the area, the requirement will be for archaeologists to undertake the work of excavation. Excavation, although it will involve delay to the scheme, should not be seen simply as an extra burden on parishes. The knowledge learned through an excavation can indeed be of positive benefit to a parish by adding to what is known about the history and development of the church and putting the building and the parishioners into a much wider context. The anxiety often expressed when human remains are exposed can be allayed through the sympathetic treatment and careful removal of the bones, ready for later reinterment elsewhere in the churchyard.

Funding archaeological work

As mentioned above, it is of utmost importance to consult the Diocesan Advisory Committee at the earliest possible stage of a new project involving disturbance of the churchyard. After such consultation, it will be possible to estimate the likely cost of any necessary archaeological work, including the writing of a report on the results, and to allow for this in the budget and fundraising activities. The earlier a proposal for development is discussed with an archaeologist, the greater the chance of avoiding expensive archaeological work.

Where a proposed project is large, such as the construction of an extension to the church, it is probable that any associated archaeological expenses will represent only a small percentage of the total costs. In these cases, the extra fundraising will not seem too onerous and it will be clear to the parish why the archaeology is necessary. Paying for archaeological work as a result of maintenance projects, such as repairing an ancient churchyard wall, may seem to the parish to be more burdensome. The expense of this type of archaeological recording, though not great in itself, may represent a larger proportion of the total costs and it may not be clear to the layperson why the work is necessary. Such recording is important however and, when combined with other sources of evidence, can tell us much about the past. If there is any confusion in the parish as to why archaeological work needs to be done prior to a scheme, the Diocesan Archaeological Adviser will be able to explain the reasons.

If the disturbance is to be caused as a result of necessary repairs grant-aided by English Heritage, their grant may sometimes be extended to help offset archaeological costs. There may be local sources of funding for archaeology, about which the Diocesan Archaeological Adviser will be able to advise. Costs may be offset by using archaeologists as subcontractors for the excavation element of the project so ensuring that the final bill, though higher than if no archaeological intervention were required, is not exorbitant.

Finds

The main concern of archaeologists when excavating a site is the evidence of structures and their relationships hidden under the soil, which helps to reconstruct the past. In association with these deposits, physical artefacts may be found such as coins, pottery and tools, which help both to date and to interpret the archaeological layers. Any such finds are the property of the incumbent but during a vacancy the PCC has a proprietary interest in them. Although rarely of any monetary value, they may have historical and local significance. Casual finds, for example made while grave digging, may also be of relevance to the history of the church and church-yard and should be reported to the County Archaeologist, the Diocesan Archaeological Adviser, or to an established local museum. This is important for two reasons:

1. to conserve any important finds to prevent their decay;
2. to map the discovery on the Sites and Monuments Record (SMR). Individually, finds may appear trivial, but when plotted regionally they often reveal patterns that may assist in the writing of more accurate history.

All finds are subject to the faculty jurisdiction and therefore a faculty must be obtained before any substantive work (other than recording) is carried out on them or before they are removed from the site.

Human remains

It is very likely that an excavation (whether archaeological or otherwise) within a churchyard will reveal human remains. While care should always be taken to avoid damage to all archaeological deposits, in the case of human remains the reasons for preservation *in situ* go deeper than simply a desire to preserve information about the past. Ethical and theological sensitivities need also to be taken into account. The Council for the Care of Churches' Church Archaeology Working Party in 1999 made the following recom-mendations in relation to this issue:

There should be a presumption against the disturbance of human remains;

Disturbed remains should be afforded respectful treatment;

There should be a presumption in favour of reinterment of remains. (*Church Archaeology: its Care and Management*, Council for the Care of Churches, 1999, listed in the bibliog-raphy on page 144 of this book)

If human remains are to be disturbed during an excavation, good archaeological practice dictates that this should be carried out with due respect, preferably behind screens. Sometimes, but by no means always, important information can be obtained through the scientific study of human remains revealed during an archaeological excavation. If a case can be made for removing remains from the site for further study, they should eventually be re-interred unless a very convincing case can be made for an alternative course of action.

Monuments and conservation

Gravestones, monuments and tombs can give us both archaeological and documentary evidence (from inscriptions) about the history of a church. Some of these monuments may be so significant that they are listed in the same way as important buildings by the DCMS and fine examples can be found in many ancient churchyards. It is important to record such monuments as part of a wider churchyard plan (see below and Appendix 1). It is also a good idea to make a phased plan for their conservation so that they do not become neglected to the point of collapse. It should be noted that conservation and repair work to monuments, especially to larger examples and table tombs, can have archaeological implications in the same way as work to the fabric of the church itself. In more

fig. 17
Eighteenth-
century head-
stones at
Parson Drove,
Cambridgeshire.

© Christopher Dalton

complex cases, a conservator should be employed for such repairs though a skilled memorial mason may well be competent for more straightforward work. In any event, the Diocesan Archaeological Adviser should be informed of any conservation work planned for such tombs.

Alterations

There is often a need to change some fundamental aspect of a churchyard in order to serve the present day needs of the parish and wider community. This might be the construction of new path-ways, access for the disabled, the addition of lighting, the setting aside of an area for cremated remains, or even the creation of a car park. All of these projects will produce to a greater or lesser extent a change in overall appearance, and it is wise to consider carefully the visual impact that will result: for example it is no longer accepted practice to remove *in situ* grave markers simply to 'tidy up' a churchyard. Some yards contain important landscape features such as trees, planted borders, paths, and areas left deliberately 'wild'. If these features are the result of deliberate and careful plan-ning in the past, then it will be necessary to consider the merits of retaining or reinstating these historic 'garden' features.

Recording

Churchyards may contain a great number of diverse features, some relating to past uses, others to present functions, all in addition to the obvious number of graves and grave-markers. These features will not all be apparent at first glance. It is therefore wise to pre-pare an accurate and detailed drawn plan to enable the parish to understand the churchyard better and to plan its development. The Diocesan Archaeological Adviser will be able to give useful advice, if not practical help.

Making a plan

It is important on every account to keep a full and accurate record of all burials in the churchyard. New burials will not immediately have a grave-marker, and old gravestones may have to be moved temporarily for repair or access, and it is only with the aid of an accurate plan that such graves may be positively identified when not otherwise marked on the ground. There will be many old graves whose positions cannot be identified simply by looking, although mounds and depressions may yield clues as to their location. These should all be plotted on the churchyard plan along with grave-markers, monuments, kerbstones, and areas set aside for cremated remains, plus, of course, the church itself. The boundary features of the yard such as hedges, fences, trees, and gates need to be included, as do paths, both hard-surfaced and mown grass. It may not seem important today to have such accurate detail, but it may pay dividends to the next generation who take over the management of the churchyard and who will need to know these things. A guide to making a churchyard plan is included in Appendix 1.

chapter 10

The living churchyard

The churchyard landscape

What should a churchyard look like? This simple question encapsulates the issues in churchyard care, particularly for the living elements. The grass, the trees, the birds determine much of the character of a churchyard, not to mention the splash of colour from flowers and the patina of lichens on the graves. The answer will depend on your point of view. So many people have a stake in churchyards, from bereaved families to local authorities, and they all want different things from the churchyard. The task of PCCs and others with responsibility for churchyards is to handle these expectations through careful design. Professional landscape architects and ecologists can help and parishes should be prepared to spend money on their services, just as they would on an architect for the church itself. The following seven-step procedure is suggested as an easy way of ensuring everything is considered.

The practice of churchyard care: a seven-step procedure

1. Agree aims

All other decisions will flow from achieving a shared understanding of what a particular churchyard is for and what it should look like. How are differing views, held with distinctive strengths in each particular parish, to be accommodated? Where they conflict, imaginative lateral thinking may be the answer, or at least suggest a compromise. Can different aims be pursued in different areas of the churchyard? How should its history be continued and what should be kept and what discarded from its current design?

There are certain general aims that must be considered.

The churchyard should be a fitting place for burial

Churchyards carry great emotional weight. They are places designated for dead people to be buried but they can also enable the living to find God. The character of a churchyard will help or hinder people in their approach to God and in their coming to terms with death. They are also a crucible for working out our relationship with nature, which is undergirded by God, and for coming to terms with time. The churchyard represents continuity with the past, experiences continual change, and allows hope for the future. Many people desire tidiness in the churchyard but excessive tidiness can represent a sort of fear in the face of death. Allowing the plants to flower and to set seed is a symbol of hope in new life and in God's gift of resurrection. One aspect of so-called green burials is the growing popularity of woodland burials, where trees are planted around graves. This will not normally be possible in established churchyards, but parishes and dioceses should consider whether new land ought to be made available for this. In Ely diocese the diocesan authorities have encouraged the creation of a woodland cemetery by the Arbory Trust outside Cambridge. It will be interesting to see how easy it will prove in the future to attend to both ecological principles and to mourners' sensitivities.

Wildlife conservation is a high priority

The last two decades of the twentieth century saw a gathering revolution in popular attitudes towards nature conservation, and the churchyard has come into focus as one of our most important national assets in terms of the habitat it provides for a wide range of grasses, mosses, lichens, ferns, fungi, flowers, trees (both native and introduced), insects, reptiles, birds and mammals. When there have been so many developments in agriculture and so much building, the churchyard has remained a sanctuary where once common plants and animals can still be found. Churchyards also contain habitats such as grassland, stonework and veteran trees that are quite distinctive, and unusual species find a home in them. These form our natural heritage and, once lost, cannot be put together again.

To talk of nature conservation worries many people. Will the churchyard become untidy so that it seems disrespectful to the dead? The answer is certainly 'no' if the conservation programme is well run. Some patches of grass may be left to grow longer but can remain neat-looking if the edges are kept well trimmed while most areas of grass will remain short. Most of the steps in caring for wildlife will be found to enhance the beauty of the churchyard, as they encourage more flowers, more butterflies, more birds. However, changes in management must be introduced carefully, with explanation and enthusiasm, and at an acceptable pace.

The historic landscape design should provide the framework for any new work

In many parishes the churchyard will be the site of longest dedicated land use and its boundaries will be related to ancient settlement patterns. A yew tree may be older than the church building itself, and even less venerable trees may be remnants of earlier landscaping. The history of planting is much less well known or appreciated than the history of church architecture, which is all the more reason to preserve designs from the past so that we can learn from them in the future. Even the grass is a historic feature if it retains the composition and character once typical, prior to the closer mowing begun in the eighteenth century. A richly diverse grass sward should be preserved for the sake of history, if not of nature.

The appearance and security of the churchyard must be accommodated

The churchyard provides a setting for the church building and for the tombs it contains and so it is also an architectural space. Its design should enhance these structures, just as they provide different focuses within the churchyard. The churchyard must provide suitable access to the church, with clear and safe paths for example, but it must also provide sufficient security for it. This may mean ensuring that the building is exposed to public view while any hedges may need to be thick and perhaps spiny (as also under vulnerable windows), to discourage unwanted visitors. These concerns should not be allowed to spoil the quality of the churchyard.

2. Gather information

Know your churchyard! We would not dream of altering the church building without first understanding its history and value, or be able to do so without accurate plans. Likewise in the church-yard, the PCC needs to have access to up-to-date and precise information about it, before taking any decisions. It greatly helps in planning the design and management of a churchyard if the PCC has asked people to gather the information listed below. These details will influence decisions on aims, e.g. a rare species, a noble tree or an ancient monument will deserve protection.

Information to gather

- A map showing the main features, preferably to scale. The parish architect may be able to help with this. An Ordnance Survey map may provide a base.
- A record of the plants and animals. A local volunteer may be able to do the wild flowers, but for grasses, mosses, lichens and insects, parishes may need to ask for help, and the county Wildlife Trust is a good place to start. (Further details are contained in Chapter 2 of *Wildlife in Church and Churchyard*, listed in the bibliography on page 145 of this book.)
- A record of burials and inscriptions. Recording inscriptions can help preserve them for posterity and a local family history society may be keen to include the churchyard in its programme.
- A report on the trees. A professional report on the trees as they exist at present will be much assisted by documents recording work done to them and by dated photographs.
- A history of the churchyard. Old maps, photographs or descriptions should be gathered and any other relevant material. Combine this information with the evidence visible on the ground to write a brief history of the churchyard.

3. Conceive a design

In drawing up a plan for what each part of the churchyard should look like, the designer must consider the main principles of landscape architecture. The current churchyard design may seem accidental but, like an old church, it is built up from many different elements sensitively assembled. The contributions of our generation should be fitting developments. Good design will seem so natural as not to be visible, but it will generate appropriate feelings and thoughts in those who visit or work in the churchyard. For example, a churchyard enclosed by tall trees may feel safe, or a rounded bush planted beside a corner of the church may anchor the building visually to the ground, while a series of clipped yews will give a sense of procession up to the church entrance.

Landscape design in churchyards has been a neglected subject in recent years and should be revived. PCCs should seek professional advice since popular works on garden design can be more misleading than helpful. Diocesan Advisory Committees should be able to draw on the advice of both ecologists and landscape architects and should expect PCCs to do so as well. A second edition of the CCC's publication *Wildlife in Church and Churchyard* (see bibliography on page 145 of this book) will provide some specific advice on how to treat this aspect of churchyards. Good design depends, however, on the art of understanding the site and its potential more than on knowledge and planning techniques.

4. Draw up a management plan

A sensible management plan sets out the details of how the aims are to be achieved. It may list a programme of work to the trees or establish a regime for cutting the grass at different times of the year. It may include a map, noting the treatment to be given to the different areas, such as long or short grass or the height of hedges. It should also draft a planting scheme so that those who wish to plant a tree or bush in memory of someone can be appropriately guided.

The management plan must be realistic about resources – not just money, but particularly the availability of volunteer labour. A regular churchyard gang may develop a strong sense of identity, as much as a choir. Alternatively, many churches find asking people to come to help on just two or three days a year can generate a great sense of occasion. The Community Service Order programme can be a great help if there is sufficient supervision for the people on the Order. Grants may be available, whether from public funding or from trusts, but the situation changes rapidly and parishes should seek advice from their Diocesan Advisory Committee. A wise PCC will be setting aside fee income for burials and monuments, as well as donations, to build up a capital fund, the interest from which may help pay for churchyard care as volunteers become scarcer.

Looking after a churchyard with wildlife in mind takes more reflection and a little more work than applying familiar gardening and tidying techniques. It is hard work to cut grass like a hay meadow. It requires attention to fix the best day to make the cut.

So plans should not be too ambitious at first or else interest will quickly be lost.

Rules of thumb to protect and enhance wildlife in churchyards

These practices should help PCCs to avoid common problems but they are not hard and fast rules:

- Maintain long established patterns of management.
- Avoid the use of chemicals (fertilizers, pesticides or herbicides).
- Remove grass cuttings, preferably after they have lain a few days.
- Leave small plants and lichens on walls and monuments.
- Remove woody plants from walls and monuments.
- Keep bonfires and compost heaps well sited, away from trees and good grass.
- Plant trees for the future, but with caution.

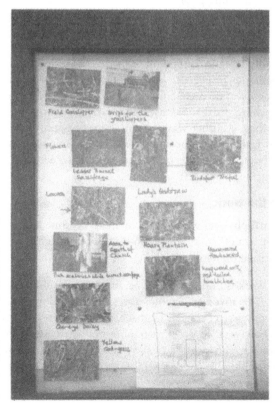

fig. 18
A display explaining how the churchyard is managed with wildlife in mind, together with photographs of its natural history treasures.

© Nigel Cooper

- Inspect trees annually.
- Do not dig graves close to trees.
- Maintain established pollarding regimes.
- Seek advice on surveying and caring for the churchyard.
- Maintain an inventory of the churchyard's wild and cultivated species.

5. Explain the policy

Those responsible for churchyard management need all the support they can get in what may sometimes seem a thankless task. This can be encouraged by explaining what is being done and why. Local people can become enthusiastic over their churchyard if they are helped to realize the wealth of nature and history it contains.

One simple step is to display the map of the management plan in the church porch or somewhere similar. Even better is a fuller display, including photographs, of what to look for and how it is being cared for. This can find its way into print in the parish magazine, perhaps through a regular column, or in the church guide book or parish website. If an area that is being managed for wildlife might be thought untidy by some, a temporary notice, explaining what is going on, can be erected. It is better not to label it a 'conservation area' since that can be misleading. Ideally the whole churchyard is a conservation area, the short grass as much as the long. Another way of gaining local support is to arrange guided walks about the churchyard when the public can learn not only about the features of interest but about the way the church-yard is being managed.

6. Do the work

The hard physical work has actually to be done and not just thought about! In its own way, this labour should be honoured for its spiritual dimension.

While work is in progress, proper attention should be paid to safety issues. This involves planning the safest procedures and possibly training where chemicals or machinery are involved. People should also know what to do in cases of minor accidents or major emergencies, e.g. the location of the first aid kit or nearest telephone. PCCs should also check the insurance position for their workers and volunteers.

7. Review progress

However much planning goes into a scheme, there will be many departures from it as the work is carried out. Learning from that experience is part of the process. It is also important to monitor the impact of what is done, particularly on the wildlife. Ideally key species should be monitored every year and the whole churchyard examined every five to see whether what is being done is having the desired effect, and to revise the management plan accordingly.

Trees and shrubs

It would be hard to overestimate the importance of trees in churchyards. They are the main contributors to the design of the landscape and by their grace and disposition they provide dignity and beauty to the churchyard. A recent survey in towns has found that churchyards accommodate the oldest trees and have on average a greater covering of trees than any other type of site. The trees are the living legacy of our forebears and are evidence of their conception of what churchyards should look like. Many churchyard trees are of great age, especially the yews which, though hard to date accurately, may in a few cases be 2,000 years old or more, and thus older than the medieval building beside them.

Trees also offer important habitats for animals. They provide food and shelter for insects; for example the Holly Blue butterfly requires both holly and ivy to complete its life cycle. Likewise birds feed on their berries as well as on the insects on the tree. Different trees provide nesting sites for different species of birds; so robins, gold-crests and tits enjoy yews while finches and thrushes prefer shrubs. A churchyard with tall trees may be the home of a rookery, now much less common than they were. In some places birds can be encouraged by the provision of nest boxes but these need to be cleaned and repaired at the end of each season. Old trees with hollows may provide roosts for bats and these may be of different species (e.g. noctules) from those roosting in the church. They are legally protected from disturbance. Even when a tree dies, it may remain important for the habitat, especially since standing dead timber is so rare these days. Really old trees have recently been recognized as of immense conservation importance for rare beetles, fungi, lichens and other organisms that are found only in these veteran trees.

Planting trees

It is a common misconception that planting a tree is always an environmentally friendly act. To plant a tree can spoil a distinctive habitat and reduce it to the humdrum. The habitat in churchyards most deserving of conservation is grassland and no trees should be planted that would shade significant areas of grass; survey first if necessary. Trees can damage other things too, e.g. buildings, monuments or archaeological features. There are special regulations for trees near highways and rivers which involve consultation with the local planning authority. Trees planted now can reduce room for church extensions or burials in future years. Because mistakes are easily made over planting decisions, dioceses should require PCCs to obtain a faculty or at least to consult the archdeacon.

As long as these warnings are heeded, it is often appropriate to plant trees, either to conserve an old design feature for the next generation or for some new purpose. Care should be taken to consider the impact of the new tree on the appearance of the churchyard when it is full grown, as well as choosing an appropriate species. It may be more satisfactory to move a naturally generating tree than to buy one from a nursery.

Checklist before planting a tree
- Is there a landscape design for the churchyard? Does the proposed tree fit this design? Will the mature tree obscure views or dominate, or be too small in scale?
- Is there a historic planting scheme? Would the proposed tree aid the conservation of this scheme?
- Does the species fit the site? Should it be a native or an exotic? Should it stand out from neighbouring trees by being decorative or striking? Is there a history of plant disease on the site? Are the soil and climate suitable? Is the tree specimen of local genetic stock?
- Would the proposed tree be too close to the building, posing a threat to the foundations, roofs or underground services? Would it be too close to boundary walls, monuments, a river bank or the highway?
- Would excavating for planting or the growing tree's roots pose a threat to archaeological remains and deposits?
- Would it impede any future extension to the church or a detached hall?

fig. 19
Trees planted over the last three centuries as part of evolving churchyard design.

© Nigel Cooper

- Will it significantly reduce the area for future burials?
- Will it shade grassland, headstones, ponds or damp areas? A botanical survey may be needed to assess their relative importance. Would it compete with a veteran tree?
- Is it a species that is known to cause problems, e.g. by sending out penetrating roots or by producing poisonous fruit?
- Are there naturally regenerating trees present that would thrive better than a planted one?
- Is the PCC aware of the recommended good practice for the planting and aftercare of young trees? (Keep free of grass and weeds; water when it has not rained for two weeks; remove stakes after two growing seasons; keep strimmers well away.) Young trees establish best unless there is danger of vandalism. There is no point planting a tree to let it die.

Threats to trees

A tree's root system is not a mirror image of the branching system above ground. A tree is much more like a wineglass attached to a napkin. The roots are largely shallow, mostly in the top metre (though some reach 3 m), and they extend well beyond the dripline, up to three times the canopy's diameter. The thick roots close to the trunk base form the root plate which is important in providing a fulcrum to prevent tilting, the force of the leaning tree being resisted by tension in the root system. If roots in tension are cut there is a danger that the tree will start to lean. The thick roots are not significantly replaced if cut and all their branches will also be lost. Trees can usually tolerate about 20 per cent loss of their rooting system, though there is cumulative damage if more than one hole is dug. If a trench is being dug, the minimum distance from trees should be 12 m (39 ft) for mature trees, according to BS 5837:1991. Roots over 25 mm (1 in) diameter should not be cut. Grave pits are not as damaging to tree roots as continuous trenches but often graves are being dug far too close to trees. There should be no digging at all in the vicinity of veteran trees (including old yews); current guidance is no nearer than 5 m (16 ft) outside the dripline or within a radius of 15 times the diameter of the tree at breast height, whichever is the greater.

New buildings and car parks pose a serious threat to established trees. Trees may be stressed or killed by damage to their roots from altering soil levels and compaction, constructing paths and laying services. For details see the British Standard BS 5837 *Code of Practice for Trees in Relation to Construction*.

Often trees fall under suspicion when cracks appear in buildings. Water extraction by tree roots may indeed be the cause, but the soil beneath an old church will be too dry and compacted to tempt many roots to grow there. It must be clearly established that a tree really is to blame before permission is given to fell it. Engineers are too ready to recommend tree felling rather than considering if there may be other causes for the cracks or whether the cracks can be tolerated. Diocesan Advisory Committees should require long-term level monitoring and evidence from soil pits of shrinkable clay and living roots (see *Tree Root Damage to Buildings* by G. Biddle, listed in the bibliography on page 145 of this book).

Churchyard yews may be very ancient, but they are not the only veteran trees that require attention and care. All old trees are valuable. Their antiquity is venerable, their form picturesque and they provide unique and scarce habitats. The main threat to them is not decay but human interference. In particular, hollow trunks and a half-dead appearance create safety worries; and yet it was often much younger and apparently sound trees that fell during the hurricanes of 1987 and 1990, while the hollow veterans stood firm. Expert advice is needed to choose the right solution. Pollarding or coppicing prolongs the life of a tree so long as it is started early and continued regularly. Often this has been neglected in recent decades and so there may be debate on whether to resume it or not.

Old trees should be treated with particular respect. Keep them free of ivy, elders and brambles, and do not let trees around them get to any size; do not attach notices or fences or drive in nails; do not surround them with concrete or stone pavements or structures, or let cars park under them or otherwise let the soil get compacted, e.g. by a new path; don't pile up compost, soil, stones or rubbish over their roots or in hollow cavities; do not let mowers or strimmers ever touch the tree. Bonfires are particularly harmful, as they may kill not only the branches but also the trunk bark, leading to an infection and the eventual death of the tree. However, storm damage and naturally occurring fungi may even prove beneficial – take advice. Where wood falls off an old tree, it should be retained as near as possible to the place where it fell. It is best not to remove the leaf litter in the autumn.

Inspections and record keeping

Trees should be inspected regularly to ensure that they contain no apparent sources of danger such as a broken branch likely to fall; any remedial action discovered to be necessary must be carried out promptly. Unless there is cause for concern, it is not essential for tree inspections to be carried out by a professional, but the inspector's knowledge must be greater than that of a country person not practically concerned with tree care. If there is difficulty in finding someone suitably skilled, it may be necessary to pay for outside advice. It is becoming evident that an occasional survey by professionals is advisable.

How often to carry out such inspections and to what level, are questions that will depend on the risk of harm and damage from churchyard trees, although an annual inspection is most common. That in turn will depend on relevant circumstance, such as the age, species and condition of the trees, the number of people and vehicles passing by, and whether children are likely to be put at risk. Particular care must be taken where trees are close to a well-used path, either in or adjacent to the churchyard, or to a road, or to any other much-used facility such as a school, car park, playground or the garden of a public house. Because accidents would affect a number of people, the courts are likely to take a tougher stance if there is evidence of any breach of duty of care. Quite apart from this legal liability, how would congregations feel if, through negligence in caring for their trees, property was damaged or someone injured or killed? The Church should set a good example.

On the other hand, there is increasing recognition that trees, especially veteran ones, deserve protection not condemnation if they pose hazards. The way forward is to reduce the risk, not necessarily the hazard. One obvious way to do this is to route pedestrians away from such trees (an example of managing the target not the tree). Also, trees with rot may not be as liable to failure as once thought. A PCC should produce a written safety policy which sets out to balance the historic, environmental and amenity value of trees with their associated risks. It should also state that non-tree management options should be considered first.

Inspection should cover both trees and 'targets', i.e. what is there to be damaged (people and property) and how often it is present. Examination of trees is best done in the early autumn, when fungi are most obvious and any early leaf fall is noticeable. Further guidance is available in Chapter 7 of *Wildlife in Church and Churchyard* (see bibliography, page 145), but tree inspections are becoming more and more professional and those who conduct them should have read *Principles of Tree Hazard Assessment and Management* by Lonsdale and *Veteran Trees: a guide to risk and responsibility* from English Nature. Details of both these publications are given in the bibliography on page 145 of this book. Regular inspection will show where trees could cause damage to buildings, paths and graves or pose a risk to people, and how to take appropriate preventive action. This will also help with planning and budgeting, saving money in the longer term.

Surgery, pollarding and felling

Minor work on trees can be undertaken by the parish, without any requirement for diocesan permission (though that of the local authority may be necessary), including formative pruning such as taking out weak forks and selecting a leader, shortening wide-sweeping laterals, removing crossing branches and dead shoots and also crown-lifting as the tree grows taller. Split, hanging or dead branches that are small and in easy reach can be removed.

When pruning, it is essential not to damage the branch bark ridge and the branch collar. If you do not recognize these features consult an up-to-date book. Pruning of young trees should be done when they are dormant; sealants should not be used over wounds. The exception is when there is a risk of silver leaf infection. Pruning trees is more complex than is often realized and volunteers must make sure they know what they are doing. Badly pruned trees can generate hazards in the future and so a liability of negligence.

Felling and more substantial lopping and topping will normally require a faculty. In addition, almost any work to a tree that is the subject of a tree preservation order requires the consent of the local planning authority; and six weeks' notice must be given to the authority before a tree is touched if the tree is in a conservation area. Consent to fell a tree, either from the chancellor or from the planning authority, may be subject to a condition that a replacement tree is planted. Further, if the tree is old or has small cavities, it may contain bats or other protected species, and English Nature should be involved as early as possible.

For such work it is important to use well-trained tree surgeons who are sufficiently insured rather than passing traders who offer to do the job cheaply. The local authority may hold a list of qualified people as does the Arboricultural Association. Contractors should work to British Standard 3998:1989.

Contractors should draw up both a specification and a method statement as well as a price, which should be checked by the diocese, either through the archdeacon or the Diocesan Advisory Committee. If the stump is to be removed, this should be planned from the outset. PCCs can now sell the timber from the churchyard and should check with the surgeon as to the timing and method of felling to obtain the best value for the timber, perhaps as veneer timber. Clippings from yew trees and hedges are also currently valuable as a source of the cancer drug, Taxol.

Hedges

The boundaries of a churchyard are frequently ancient and any hedges that mark them may share in this antiquity and should be protected. The age of a hedge may be discovered by examining old maps and parish records and, in some circumstances, by the diversity of woody species along its length. Old hedges are also valuable for the wealth of wildlife they house, from the plants at their base to the birds nesting in the branches. Agricultural hedges may be protected by the local authority and the faculty system should also protect churchyard hedges that are old or rich in wildlife.

There are many different styles of hedge. Some are trimmed, some are kept informal like a field hedge, while others are coppiced, i.e. periodically cut to ground level and allowed to regrow. The traditional management of a hedge is best continued unless it is very out of place. For maximum natural history interest, each side of a hedge should be cut only once every two years; this allows flowers and fruit to form and insect eggs to hatch and grow. The hedge should be approximately A-shaped and left to grow to over 2 m (6 ft 6 in) high if possible, as it encourages many more bird species to nest than a lower one. Hedge bottoms should be left thick with a strip of long grass beside them. The best time to cut a hedge is late winter since it retains berries for winter food but avoids disturbing nesting birds.

Old hedges can become gappy as plants die. There is little room for natural regeneration if the hedge bottom has been kept too tidy. New specimens to be inter-planted into the hedge have to be helped to survive the competition from the existing plants by the creation of a weed-free gap one metre (3 ft) wide. It is best to use transplants protected by tree shelters. Alternatively the hedge can be layered. In this technique the hedge is coppiced except for one or two stems from each stool which are retained but cut three-quarters through near the base. These stems are then bent over, fastened down and some soil is put over the stem where it touches the ground. In many cases it will root here and come to form a new stool. Plashing or laying involves weaving the stems together rather than getting them to root in the ground. New hedge trees can be planted in the same way as hedge infills, or self-sown plants can be selected and, escaping the hedge cutter, allowed to grow into mature trees – often with a characterful shape at the bottom as a reminder of their early days of struggle in the hedge.

Whether planting a new hedge or infilling an old one, there is the question of which species to plant. Old hedges often contain a great diversity of species and this pattern can be followed or replaced by planting a single species such as hedgerow hawthorn. The advantage of the latter is that it lacks the pretence of the former in mimicking an ancient hedge. However, many people prefer mixed planting. If this is chosen, species common in local hedges should be used.

This advice applies to what might be termed country hedges. In more formal situations, different considerations apply and the desired design effect is uppermost. Leyland cypress hedges are popular as they are fast growing and dense but they should be avoided in churchyards – they quickly become too tall to be topped easily and their uniform colour and texture are unattractive. Other more desirable options are too numerous to mention.

Grassland

With the ploughing up or spraying of old meadowland, many meadow flowers have become very dependent on churchyards for survival. The Nature Conservancy Council estimated in the 1980s that about 98 per cent of herb-rich meadowland had been lost over the previous 30 years. In lowland counties, some meadow flowers have as much as 50 per cent of their surviving population in churchyards. Not just the individual species, but the grassland as a whole is under threat from the forces of modern development. Churchyards retain a herb-rich grassland that historically was once widespread and can be thought of as a little remnant of the pre-eighteenth-century countryside. This makes grassland the habitat of greatest importance in a churchyard and heightens the debate over its management. The principles of grassland conservation may need to be tempered with what is acceptable locally and with what labour is available, but the conservation of the habitat itself remains the priority, especially where the grassland is particularly rich in species. Sceptics may be convinced by the visual delight of a flower-rich grass sward.

fig. 20
Flowers in
the grass.

© Nigel Cooper

At the turn of the twentieth to the twenty-first century, churchyard grass is being lost in novel ways. Many churches are having extensions built or hard standings constructed for cars. To reduce damp, ground levels around buildings are being lowered. Each of these developments destroys some grassland. Diocesan Advisory Committees should check the quality of the grass that would be affected by such schemes, asking the parish to make a survey if appropriate. If the grassland is of conservation value, the scheme should be resited in a less sensitive place or perhaps the turfs should be moved and relaid.

Basics of grassland care

(Greater detail is set out in Chapter 3 of *Wildlife in Church and Churchyard* – see page 145 of this book.)

1. Maintain traditional management

Where a particular pattern of grass cutting is long established, such as being cut frequently and short or left long and cut annually, the plants and animals living there will be suited to that regime. In these cases, any changes in cutting regimes should be introduced cautiously. It is essential to survey what is already growing and living there and to assess its conservation importance before risking any change that might threaten its survival. However, where there have been many changes in management over the recent past, a survey may help to indicate a suitable cutting regime for the plants and wildlife already there. The grass will need to be left long for one season to enable its principal features to be identified.

Most churchyards have long been mechanically mown but a few are still grazed, generally by sheep. Grazing is ideal for some types of grassland when the stocking density is right or for a short period following a hay cut. It involves a lot of work and the cooperation of a friendly farmer but it not only has survived but has been reintroduced by some parishes. The local Wildlife Trust may be able to give advice.

2. Remove cuttings

In the garden it is common practice to fertilize the soil to improve growth but in the churchyard increased soil fertility is bad for conservation. The added nutrients make it possible for vigorous grasses and other plants to grow which compete with and eliminate the scarcer plants adapted to less nutrient-rich habitats. It is for this reason that grass cuttings should be removed to prevent the nutrients within them restoring fertility. Clods of mashed grass from rotary mowers will smother plants and look unsightly and so, like fallen leaves, should be taken away. Cuttings ideally should be allowed to lie for about a week before being collected. This allows time for seeds to fall out of the cuttings and for any insects to move away.

fig. 21
This clump of grass cuttings is unsightly and damaging.

© Nigel Cooper

3. Use no chemicals

Lawn treatments are particularly damaging. The herbicides will kill many of the interesting broad-leaved plants and the fertilizer will encourage vigorous grasses that will require more cutting. Lawn mosses can also be very diverse in churchyard grass and should not be treated in an attempt to kill them.

4. Diversify grass height

Most churchyards already have a diversity of grass cutting regimes, with some grass cut short regularly while other areas are left to grow longer. Different species of plants and animals are suited to different regimes so that, put simply, the more varied the height of the grass, the more species there will be. Some animals and insects, e.g. butterflies, are particularly attracted to the boundaries between different lengths of grass. Priority must be given to those habitats already well established – and this may be short grass in the case of churchyards – so it may be better for conservation to aim for just a moderate increase in diversity.

Besides nature conservation, there are also human issues. Is there sufficient labour to cut the grass according to the ideal regime? Is long grass visually acceptable? It is not appropriate to have long grass about the entrance to the church, around regularly visited graves or where the wedding photographs are taken. Yet long grass can be made to look tidy and cared for if edges and paths are kept cut and trimmed back. Sometimes the area chosen to grow long is selected purely because of the flowers in it. It is often a good idea if the patches are carefully shaped and symmetrically positioned, like island beds in a lawn. Paths should be wide, perhaps two metres, so that grass does not fall over them.

5. Remember the animals

Grassland of different heights provides homes for many types of animal. These will include snails and voles as well as insects. Slow-worms are vulnerable when the grass is being cut as they may not move out of the way: keep a lookout. The timing of grass cuts is particularly critical for insects, depending on the species. For example, a cut in June can almost eliminate butterflies from a site as the food is removed for caterpillars, shelter for pupae, and the adults lose sources of nectar and also territory markers, courtship posts, roosting sites and the visual clues on where to lay the next generation of eggs. Staggering the timing of the cut may help. Try to enroll the assistance of an entomologist to determine what species are present and how best to care for them.

Rabbits and moles are often thought of as nuisances. Neither is easily eradicated. They can be beneficial to other wildlife; molehills provide patches of bare soil where seeds can germinate. (It is best to press new molehills back into the ground rather than removing the spoil, which leads to increasing unevenness of the ground.)

6. Be cautious over introductions

It is a current fashion to introduce new species of plants into grassland but this is rarely appropriate in churchyards unless the sward is particularly species-poor, as it may be in towns and cities. If it is decided to do so, only species and seed typical to that locality should be used. It is not easy to establish plants in a grass sward; sowing into molehills is one idea, planting out pot-grown plants another. Where the grass is very vigorous, parasitic species like yellow rattle, or lousewort where it is damp, may reduce its vigour and allow other species to increase.

7. Monuments

Where there are many monuments, especially those with kerbs, it is very difficult to cut the grass satisfactorily. Where such an area is currently cut short, every effort should be made to continue this level of care. Once such areas have become neglected it is hard work to bring them back to looking tidy. It is tempting to give such areas just an annual cut, but then mowing may damage many of the monuments hidden in the grass and vice versa. Such areas are often overgrown with rank and weedy vegetation and have limited wildlife value. To call them conservation areas gives conservation a bad name.

In country areas grave mounds may still be common. These also create work for churchyard managers, but they are often of wildlife value. The accelerated drainage on the mounds and the differing lengths of grass encourage a different selection of plants. They are also favourite sites for ants to build their nests as the mounds help raise the nests into the warm sunlight.

Walls and monuments

In the lowland counties of England few natural exposures of rock remain and the ancient walls of churchyards have become an important substitute for many species of rock-loving plants. The plants of the first stages of colonization are the rarest and, fortunately, least likely to damage the walls and monuments on which they grow. For further information see Chapter 4 in *Wildlife in Church and Churchyard*; details of this publication are given in the bibliography on page 145 of this book.

It is convenient to distinguish three degrees of plant growth on stonework. These roughly correspond to the stages of colonization of the stonework over time:

1. Mosses, liverworts and lichens. Although most people cannot identify the many different species, they can appreciate the distinctive patterns created by the colours and textures of each species and their spread over the surfaces. A high priority should

fig. 22
Lichens on a headstone.

© Nigel Cooper

be given to preserving these species, some of which are virtually restricted to churchyards, and provide habitats for tiny animals. Whenever there is a potential threat to these plants from a proposed operation, an expert should be commissioned to survey the area. There may have to be finely balanced decisions weighing the need to conserve the structural integrity of a monument against the claims of a species on the surface.

2. Ferns and small herbaceous plants and grasses. These plants may colonize the mortar joints, and where the roots remain small and soft, they cause no damage to structures.
3. Woody-rooted plants. These damage structures and should be removed. They include sapling trees, bushes and tough perennials. Ivy is a special case because, while it can cause damage, sometimes it already has such a hold of a wall that it is practically holding the wall together; it is also of great value to wildlife, providing winter food and shelter. A compromise is to prevent ivy growing over new surfaces but to trim it back from time to time where it is already established.

Pointed walls

Different stonework habitats require different treatments. Pointed walls will need to be repointed from time to time. When this is necessary, lime mortars should be used. This is best for ancient walls not only architecturally, but ecologically too: lime mortar is most readily colonized by the plants and animals of interest. To preserve harmless plants repointing should be undertaken in small, scattered patches. A careful watch should be kept that woody-rooted plants do not become established on walls or at their bases but avoid routine spraying which could kill other valuable plants as well.

Monument faces

Monuments should also be protected from woody plants. Ivy is a particular issue, and along with damage from its roots, the way it retains water (which may become acidic) tends to damage the surface of monuments, making them more susceptible to weathering when they are eventually exposed. Ivy should not be directly pulled off monuments, but killed first by being cut at the base. Tombstone lichens tell an important story and should be preserved. Some families may wish to keep their headstones clean, but those who are recording inscriptions in a churchyard should be discouraged from removing extensive patches of lichens, which will anyway hasten the loss of the inscriptions. The lichens growing on a stone are adapted to the compass direction they face and the degree of slope, so will be harmed if the monument is moved. If the grass or shrubs are allowed to grow tall persistently, their shade will also affect the lichens.

The base of monuments

It is not easy to mow or graze close to a monument and so the grass at the base tends to be allowed to grow tall and is only cut once a year with shears. For this reason, and because of the influence of the stone on the soil around it, the plants can be distinctive here, for instance lesser calamint is largely restricted to this habitat.

Two new ways of keeping this awkward area tidy seem convenient but cause problems in the long term: strimming and spraying can damage the stones and hasten weathering. By keeping the vegetation permanently short, strimming alters its character; spraying with herbicides around the base creates a ring of bare soil but the spray may damage the stone, as well as killing the plants around and on the stone. The bare soil is also vulnerable to erosion and this may lead to the undermining or tilting of the monument.

Within kerbs

The area within kerbed graves is often distinctive and can be treated as a sort of wild-flower bed. Where the ground is of soil, grassland species such as ox-eye daisy often grow to profusion and will make a fine display. Where the graves are covered with chippings over a concrete base, rock plants such as stonecrops become established. All these should be encouraged, but coarse grasses may invade, especially as the concrete base breaks up, and these should be weeded out.

Large monuments

Some monuments are large and complex and may be inaccessible behind iron railings. They provide many habitats for wildlife but can easily get out of control as brambles and saplings become established. Once a monument is damaged, it can be very expensive to repair, so good monuments should be diligently kept free of woody plants.

Geology

The great range of stones used in building our churches and chosen for monuments has made churchyards ideal places to study geology and processes such as weathering and thus offer extensive opportunities to include schools in the appreciation of churchyards. The geology of the stones also contributes to the individual character of a churchyard.

Other habitat types

Fences and gates

Wooden fences and gates are also colonized by lichens and mosses, though usually of different species from the ones on stonework. When wood is treated with preservative, these plants are killed; so, as a general rule, it is best either to keep the wood regularly treated and clean or, if it has become grown over, to allow the lichens to remain and plan to replace the wooden structure in the long term.

Paths

Grass paths are common in churchyards, varying from official public footpaths to informal tracks to groups of graves. It is important for public relations to keep these well mown and their edges trimmed. Well-trampled paths may have distinctive plants growing in them. If they are so well used that they tend to become muddy, it is probably appropriate to give them a gravel surface. Here a certain degree of mud between the shingle can be tolerated by walkers which can give the opportunity for specially adapted plants, some increasingly rare such as cudweeds. Alternatively the gravel may be colonized by mosses, which may also include rare species. Because of their botanical interest, gravel paths should not be paved without a survey to check first. They can remain working paths by adding more shingle, rolling or cutting the path or the careful use of a non-persistent weedkiller in rotating patches. Decaying tarmac paths can mimic gravel surfaces and can house interesting grasses. Paved and brick paths may have significant plants growing in the cracks and mosses may live where the surface is frequently damp. Invertebrates may live under the stones and reptiles and amphibians hide beneath them.

Flower beds and graves

Shortly after bereavement many families wish to treat the grave as a sort of flower bed. Anything that helps the grief process is valuable and this kind of gardening should be accepted in principle. It is wise for PCCs to set their own rules, which might include setting maximum dimensions for such beds so that mowers can cut around the plot and discouraging the planting of bushes or other more permanent plants. As families often gradually come to neglect these graves, the rules should also permit the PCC to take over the management of the grave including putting it down to grass. This must be after consultation with the family unless it can no longer be traced. These tended graves can bring bright splashes of colour to the churchyard.

Should the PCC construct flower beds of its own? Besides the issue of the labour of maintenance, flower beds present an aesthetic question. Generally speaking, the grander the church building, the less suitable would it be to surround it with flower beds. Flower beds may be more appropriately sited away from the building, forming part of a Garden of Remembrance where cremated remains are interred.

Spoil heaps

When a grave is backfilled, not all the soil will fit. The surplus is commonly tipped beneath the nearest tree. Not only is this unsightly, but it poses a threat to the tree, making it vulnerable to rot where the bark is smothered and burying its roots. The spoil should be deposited in a carefully chosen spot.

Compost heaps

Compost heaps tend to spread as attempts are made to tidy up rubbish including floral tributes and plastic flowers casually scattered by visitors to the churchyard. A PCC needs to be firm and insist that the heap is carefully sited and delimited away from trees and that only suitable organic material is put in it. As it expands it may be possible to ask local gardeners to take the compost away for free, otherwise it may need carting away. A compost heap is not only an ecologically sound way of disposing of rubbish but provides sanctuary for wildlife. For instance it is a favourite place for slow-worms and toads feeding on the insects that live there. Its warmth makes it a good winter home for grass snakes.

Log piles

Piles of wood are also valuable for wildlife. If the wood is densely packed in a shady place, they will attract animals such as hedge-hogs. As they may hibernate here, be careful when examining the

fig. 23
A bonfire site with, in the background, the stump of a tree fatally infected after a bonfire many years ago.

© Nigel Cooper

piles over winter. If the piles are of less substantial, twiggy wood, piled up in the open, bees and other insects can burrow in the cut ends. If the wood is to be burnt, this should be done quickly before it is colonized by insects.

Bonfires

Bonfires may sometimes be necessary but they can cause a lot of damage. If they are lit too close to trees they damage them. If lit away from trees they will kill the grass beneath and it can be many years before the patch returns to normal. In the meantime, it will attract weedy plants and nettles. If a bonfire is necessary and waste cannot be composted or carted away, it must be carefully sited in one place. Working parties must not fall prey to the temptation to burn rubbish wherever it has gathered. The resulting ash should not be scattered about the churchyard, increasing the grassland's fertility, but restricted to flower beds or given away.

Waste and scrub

Waste areas are unsightly but may have a wildlife value, at least in a sunny position. Garlic and hedge mustards as well as nettles are food plants for a number of butterflies, while brambles provide food and shelter for birds. There may be places where small patches of these plants can be left. If nettles are cut in June, regrowth will allow for a second generation of caterpillars.

Where a churchyard has been neglected, woody plants such as elder, sycamore and blackthorn start to invade. This scrub is of some value to wildlife, but less than that of other churchyard habitats, so naturalists and tidy-minded gardeners can concur in removing scrub or keeping it at bay by cutting it back every few years.

Beyond the parish

Diocesan Advisory Committees

With the growing recognition of the national importance of churchyards for nature conservation and the inclusion of trees within faculty jurisdiction, Diocesan Advisory Committees are taking their responsibilities for the living churchyard increasingly seriously. To help them in this task, it is prudent to include among their membership new categories of professional: the ecologist, the arboriculturalist and the landscape architect. They should be familiar with the variety of churchyards within the diocese and their relative importance for conservation. There should at least be a Diocesan Advisory Committee member concerned especially with trees and churchyards. Such a person should try to develop a close relation-ship with the local authority's tree officer and should be given the opportunity to comment on the relevant parts of quinquennial inspection reports.

When scrutinizing proposals, Diocesan Advisory Committees should ask what impact they would have on wildlife. Even activities that at first sight have nothing to do with nature conservation may compromise it. These activities include the building of church extensions or car parks, lowering the ground level around the church building and digging trenches, repairing walls and paths, moving or repairing gravestones and monuments and tree felling and planting. All these affect more than just the trees. Diocesan Advisory Committees should hold records of planning designations relevant to churchyards such as Sites of Importance for Nature Conservation/County Wildlife Sites or equivalent. They and other bodies such as local wildlife trusts have a role in encouraging and promoting conservation, building up policies on nature conservation so that parishes can be guided in their care of the natural heritage. Last but not least, Diocesan Advisory Committees should keep abreast of the current sources of grant aid for the maintenance and conservation of churchyards. They should work together with chancellors to draw up guidance notes on trees. This should cover proposed planting schemes as well as tree surgery and tree felling. It might even be helpful if Diocesan Advisory Committees could, on occasion, offer training to parishes on how to care for trees.

Local councils

The local planning authority designates conservation areas, issues tree preservation orders and administers applications to undertake work on protected trees. Many churchyards have protected trees and for this reason and also because churchyard trees are generally so significant, local authority tree officers, busy though they are, are often willing to visit churches to give advice. Local authorities also have the power to grant-aid churchyard projects such as landscaping, conservation of tombs or tree planting.

Closed churchyards

Where a churchyard has been closed by Order in Council (see above), the PCC can require the parish or district council to maintain the churchyard. Many PCCs are relieved to relinquish responsibility, but with it also goes a loss of control. Local councils may not wish to spend money on churchyards in their care and church and parish people generally may be disappointed at what is done or not done. Even if the council is willing to take its responsibilities seriously, it may do so with different aims from those of the parish, e.g. emphasizing conservation to a greater or lesser degree. It may be better to retain responsibility and control while seeking a grant commensurate with what the council would have spent if it were maintaining the churchyard. The PCC needs to retain insurance cover in any case.

Where a district or borough council has the care of a churchyard, it will usually draw up a specification for the routine maintenance of the churchyard. This may specify things such as maximum height for the grass or how often it should be cut but such instructions may not always be appropriate for an inherently variable system of plants and animals subject to uncertain weather. It would be prudent to supply a description of the plant and animal communities to the contractors. If PCCs are themselves paying the contractors they will have a stronger voice.

Making the churchyard plan

The churchyard plan should be made at an appropriate scale which allows the location of any feature to within 300 mm (approx. 1ft imperial). The ideal scale is between 1:50 and 1:100, depending upon the size of the churchyard, but it should never be smaller than 1:250 as the important details cannot be plotted with sufficient accuracy below this. A suitable base plan of the church may already exist – the church architect may have one, or one may have been prepared in a previous quinquennial inspection – and this is a good base from which to work. The accuracy of such base plans needs to be verified, and the scale may need to be converted to that which will be used for the churchyard.

It may seem a daunting exercise to produce an accurate plan, particularly if the churchyard is large, or on sloping terrain, but expert assistance is often available, either through a surveyor member of the congregation, a local history society, or museum organization. It may well be possible to get an accurate plan produced at little or no cost through the good offices of such experts, particularly those who are interested in local history issues. However, if this does not prove possible then an approach to a local college or university surveying or archaeology department may be worth trying, as it provides a good opportunity for students to undertake practical work, though the accuracy of the end product still needs to be ensured. Finally, if no free help is forthcoming, then it may be necessary to engage a local archaeological unit which will be able to provide a useful and reliable service. Again, your Diocesan Archaeological Adviser will be able to put you in touch with suitable people. Whoever carries out the work, an accurate and detailed churchyard plan may result in the discovery of new information relating to the history and archaeology of the churchyard.

Large churchyards may contain substantial overgrown areas that hide old recumbent slabs, tree stumps, and earthworks, so it is often easier to undertake the survey during the winter months. If the survey is to be carried out in the summer, then advice may need to be sought on the advisability of clearing 'wild areas' which may be havens for rare species of flora and fauna.

It is not advisable to undertake the production of an accurate plan without expert guidance, although there is much work that can be done by the layperson to assist in these matters. A tape survey is the simplest and cheapest form of plotting the necessary details and the required tapes may be available to borrow through local schools, colleges, or architects' offices. If professional help is forthcoming, then a theodolite may be available which, in the right hands, makes surveying easier and quicker, and can result in a high degree of accuracy. Dumpy levels may be used to plot height differences in the ground level, which may be necessary on sloping sites.

The final plan must be drawn on a suitably durable material such as plastic drafting film. The lines should be inked in with a drawing pen, using a stable and lightproof pigment ink which will not fade. Copies should be produced of the plan, but it is important to update only the original as changes take place in the churchyard, and then produce new copies from this. Photocopies and dyeline prints are only semi-stable and will not last indefinitely, and it is therefore essential to store the original plan in a safe place.

Recording graves

In the recording of graves, it is most useful to allocate a unique number, or code, to each grave plotted, even if there is no visible memorial. It is wise to number in a systematic way, moving along rows from one end of the churchyard to the other. Graves may be tagged with a temporary label such as a white plastic garden tag until after the plan has been drawn up. If a grid can be superimposed on the plan, then each feature can be given a grid reference, rather like an Ordnance Survey map.

Grave-markers and monuments

These need to be recorded on a standard form, preferably at A4 size which allows easy photocopying, storage, and subsequent reading. It is a good idea to use a pencil when making the record in the churchyard as a pencil will continue to work if it is damp or raining. A neat copy should be made later in permanent black ink; in this way two original copies will have been produced. Both should be stored safely, preferably in different places in case one is subsequently destroyed. It is vital to write clearly and legibly so that there can be no confusion with later transcriptions, and where parts of the inscription on the monument are illegible this should be indicated in some consistent way on every form. Great care must be taken to ensure accuracy when copying numbers and Roman numerals, and all sides of a monument should be examined as there is often lettering to be found other than on the main face. If time and resources permit, it is a good idea to have a second person check each record in the churchyard upon completion since mistakes are easily made.

It is important to copy all visible details of grave-markers and monuments, but where the stone is partially buried it should not be excavated beyond the simple clearing of loose soil and vegetation. Remember that older monuments may have moved considerably and digging away the soil at the base may cause them to slip further and even fall. Similarly, where the face is heavily encrusted with moss or lichen, this may be serving to protect a fragile inscription; roughly uncovering the face to reveal the lettering may accelerate weathering or even cause irreversible damage.

Apart from the inscription, other information needs to be recorded such as orientation (using a compass), style of lettering, shape, decoration, and the materials from which the monument is made. The record sheet should be used in a uniform manner – codes may be employed provided that a clear key is supplied and kept with all the records. On matters of geology, it is advisable to allow someone with some expertise to complete this section – never be tempted to guess.

Photography

Each object recorded must also have a good photographic record. This is the most expensive part of the survey but is an integral part of it; it may be possible to encourage a local amateur photographer or photographic club to assist in this part of the work. A good quality 35 mm or larger format camera needs to be used since smaller negatives provide poor resolution; the ideal camera for this job is a 35 mm single lens reflex equipped with a standard 50 mm lens. Photographs need to be prepared using a slow or medium speed black and white film, i.e. between speed ISO 25 and 100; although it is tempting to use colour print film, the life of colour prints is much shorter than that of black and white. Prints should be attached to record sheets. Digital photography should not be employed to record the churchyard or any other archaeological feature.

Photographs should be taken of the churchyard and church in its setting before starting on details of individual monuments – this is extremely useful in helping to locate a particular object at a later date and may also reveal if stones have been moved. It is a very good idea to photograph all movable objects within and without the church at the same time, as such records may assist the police in recovering such items in the event of theft.

Photographs of individual monuments need to be taken face-on to the inscribed surface(s) in lighting which reveals the fullest extent of the inscription. As a general rule, the lettering should be clearly legible through the viewfinder of the camera – if not then it will probably not be legible in the subsequent photograph. The pattern of lighting makes a considerable difference to the legibility of the inscription on film, and wherever possible photographs need to be taken when oblique light (i.e. from the side) falls on the face of the monument. Often it is possible to achieve good results when sunlight strikes the side of the surface – you may have to 'follow the sun' around the churchyard during the course of a day, photographing where the best lighting occurs. Because this may result in photographs not following the numbering sequence devised for the record form, every frame should be recorded carefully in a separate notebook, and the negative and film numbers eventually copied onto the record form. Every film should be given a unique number or code – it may help to write this number on a card and photograph it as negative number one each time a new roll of film is used. It is also an idea to include the monument number in the photograph by using, for example, a small dry-wipe board or a blackboard; however it must be positioned so as not to obscure any detail.

A metric scale should be included in every photograph. A good scale may be made by cutting a length of wood to 100 mm exactly then painting 50 mm white and dividing the remaining 50 mm into equal blocks of 10 mm painted alternately black and white. Some complex memorials may require more than one photograph and the scale should appear in each one. It is better to err on the side of over-photographing if in doubt, and, to save costs, not every negative needs subsequently to be printed.

Where it is not possible to use the sun for oblique lighting, or where the inscription is heavily eroded and largely illegible to the eye, there are several solutions that may be attempted. The simplest is to provide an artificial side light, e.g. a photographic studio light, or even a simple desk lamp. However, great care must be exercised when using mains electricity outside – conditions should always be dry and an earth-leakage trip switch should be employed. Where this technique does not work or produces poor results, an electronic flash should be used, positioned between one and two metres away from the side of the stone and angled so as to illuminate the surface from a grazing angle. It may be necessary to experiment, lighting the stone from different sides and at slightly different angles; for the very best results, this should be undertaken in darkness or near darkness to eliminate the effects of 'fill-in' daylight. It is strongly advisable to have an assistant operating either the camera or the flash unit. Finally, where all else fails, there are scientific methods available to attempt to read an illegible inscription such as Laser Surface Profiling (LASP), but this is a highly specialized job and is expensive, and so should be reserved only for exceptionally important monuments.

Storing the records

Once a record has been made of a churchyard, the originals should be kept safely, preferably in the church safe. Plans should always be rolled and never folded. Further copies should be made and sent to the Diocesan Record Office and the County Sites and Monuments Record (your diocesan archivist will advise on the location of the latter); ideally a further set should be given to the local library or the county library's 'local studies collection'. Every few years new copies of the plan and copies of additional record schemes for new graves should be sent out so that all the sets are kept up to date. It is strongly advisable that the photographic negatives should be placed in archivally stable folders and deposited at the Diocesan Record Office for safe keeping.

Health and safety in churchyards

An increasing number of claims are being made against church authorities by both members of the public and churchworkers who have suffered accidents and injuries in churchyards. There are several reasons for this. There is an increased expectation among the public at large that any accident, no matter how caused, is 'someone's fault' and should result in the payment of compensation. This is fuelled by extensive coverage in the press of accidents and the subsequent awards and the aggressive advertising of legal firms who offer to undertake accident cases on a 'no win no fee' basis thus removing the possibility of any financial loss to the injured party in the pursuit of their claim.

On top of this there has been a recent plethora of health and safety legislation based on the implementation of European Directives. The Health and Safety Executive has also recently issued guidance for charity and voluntary workers indicating that it is considered good practice for 'volunteer users' to provide the same level of health and safety protection, information, instruction and training as they would in an employer/employee relationship irrespective of whether there are strict legal duties.[1]

Liability may arise under both civil and criminal law. Under civil law liability may arise as a result of negligence or a breach of the duties imposed by the Occupiers' Liability Acts of 1957 and 1984. These create a 'duty of care' which means that the incumbent, churchwardens and PCC must ensure that visitors are reasonably safe for the purposes for which they are invited or permitted to be in the churchyard – visiting or tending a grave for example. The duty of care also extends to trespassers and account must be taken of the fact that children will be less careful than adults and that child trespassers may be enticed onto land by some form of allurement and be injured as a result. A vault or tomb may appear an exciting place for a child to play or make a 'den'. It is essential, therefore, that vaults and outbuildings are kept locked or secure and any damage to tombs is repaired as quickly as possible.

Health and safety regulations come within the criminal law and a breach of these could result in prosecution, fines or even imprisonment. Churches are not exempt from health and safety law. The Local Authority Environmental Health Officers are empowered under the Health and Safety (Enforcing Authority) Regulations 1989 to enforce the Health and Safety at Work Act 1974 in places of church worship. This will include the issuing of improvement and prohibition notices as well as initiating prosecutions where they discover unsafe working practices or breach of health and safety regulations.

Reference is made in this handbook to the potential causes of accidents. By way of summary the principal ones are noted below.

Slips, trips and falls

The largest number of claims made against churches results from persons, either visitors or regular members of the congregation, slipping, tripping or falling on paths, steps or in other parts of the churchyard. A principal cause of these accidents is persons tripping over kerbs or graves that have become obscured by long grass. There is effectively no defence in such circumstances to a claim that the church authorities have failed in their duty under the Occupiers' Liability Act to ensure that visitors are reasonably safe for the purposes they were permitted to be in the churchyard.

There are references in this handbook to the length to which grass should be allowed to grow. From a health and safety standpoint, however, if there is a risk of persons tripping over kerbs or graves then grass must be kept to such a length that the kerb or grave is clearly visible. Where an area is obviously set aside as natural grassland and it does not contain any hazards that could cause injury then the need for regular cutting does not necessarily exist to the same extent.

In addition to the regular cutting of grass it is also essential that all paths, steps and car parks are regularly maintained and kept in good condition. On steep paths or steps it may be necessary to install handrails. Paths and steps used at night may require the installation of lighting. Steps leading down to boiler rooms and crypts are often without handrails or lighting and are very slippery. The top of the steps may be unprotected. The erection of railings and a gate at the top of the steps, together with the fitting of a handrail, may be necessary. The steps will also need to be regularly cleared of leaves and other debris and be treated to prevent them becoming slippery.

Gravestones that have in the past been laid as paths as well as other smooth surfaced stone paths often become extremely slippery with the accumulation of algae. These will need to be regularly cleaned to prevent the risk of slipping.

There are a number of churchyards that have no boundary wall or fence but where the churchyard is at a considerable height compared to the surrounding land. This often abuts a road and presents a risk of falls from the churchyard into the road. Consideration will need to be given as to whether or not there is a need for some means of preventing persons falling from the churchyard. Account will need to be taken of the use of the area of churchyard in question. The frequency with which it is visited, either for visiting existing graves or as a site for new burials, will determine the likelihood of the risk of some person falling.

Hazardous substances

Hazardous substances used in the churchyard will include herbicides, pesticides and petrol. You will need to record all such substances and obtain, where appropriate, copies of the manufacturers' or suppliers' hazard data sheets which detail how the substances must be stored and used, and what to do in the event of an emergency. These information sheets need to be kept close to where the substances are stored. Where possible, substitute hazardous substances with less harmful alternatives and only store sufficient for your immediate needs. Hazardous substances must be stored in proprietary containers and be clearly marked. Storage facilities must be secure. The appropriate personal protective equipment such as gloves and face masks must be available when using hazardous substances and where necessary the appropriate training given.

Plant and machinery

This will include lawnmowers, strimmers and possibly chainsaws (although their use should be discouraged) and other churchyard maintenance equipment. All equipment must be regularly examined and maintained to ensure it is safe and in good working order. The use of machinery must be restricted to those who have been properly trained. Children should not be allowed to operate machinery. Machinery must be securely locked away when not in use. Consideration needs to be given to persons working on their own with potentially dangerous machinery. Ideally no one should work alone with machinery in an isolated churchyard where it may be impossible to summon assistance in the event of an accident or injury. As a minimum anyone working alone should have a mobile phone in order to summon assistance.

Trees

There are a number of references in this handbook to the need to examine trees regularly. A constant watching brief should be maintained to look for any obviously dangerous trees or branches and a formal inspection should be carried out annually. Everything but the most minor work should be entrusted to qualified tree surgeons and in general any work on trees should not be undertaken by volunteers.

Graves

There are serious hazards arising from both the digging of graves and the leaving of open graves prior to burial. Graves must be properly shored during the digging process and be safely protected prior to burial. Detailed guidance is given in the *Code of Safe Working Practice for Cemeteries* published by the Institute of Burial and Cremation Administration.[2]

Gravestones present a hazard when they begin to lean as there is a risk of them falling and causing injury. They may need to be returned to an upright position and made secure, or laid flat. There is a tendency for tombs to subside and for the tops to slip away from the main body of the tomb or even crack. Repairs need to be undertaken as quickly as possible.

Electrical installations

All external wiring in churchyards must comply with the current Institute of Electrical Engineers Wiring Regulations. Temporary wiring should never be used, but where portable electrical equipment is being used such as electric lawnmowers, strimmers or electric drills, it should always be protected by a residual current device. Even for fixed installations such as floodlighting, where this is accessible to unskilled persons, consideration should be given to protection by residual current devices.

Floodlighting also presents other hazards. Where units are at ground level this presents a tripping hazard unless they are completely set below ground level, and then there may be a need to cover the hole with a grating or safety glass. Where floodlighting units protrude above the ground they must be clearly visible and grass must be cut around them on a regular basis. For these reasons it may be better to position floodlighting units above ground level, although this makes maintenance more difficult and presents a risk of falls from a height to those persons required to change bulbs and carry out routine maintenance. A method for undertaking these procedures will need to be established and this may require the use of some form of raised platform or hoist. Where ladders are used to access lighting units from ground level they should be secured at the base to a series of eyebolts fixed approximately two metres above ground level. Electrical systems must be isolated when any maintenance work such as light bulb changing is being carried out.

The church buildings

Hazards exist not just in the churchyard but from the church building itself. There is a risk to persons visiting or working in the churchyard from masonry or other material falling from the buildings into the churchyard. Routine examination is required of the building itself and also the land surrounding the church for evidence of falling masonry. Where this does present a risk, there is a need to fence off the area securely where there is a possibility that debris could fall, and erect appropriate warning signs.

First aid equipment and accident book

Basic first aid equipment should be available to deal with minor injuries sustained while carrying out work in the churchyard. An accident book should be available to record details of all accidents and incidents to both visitors and persons working in the churchyard. Details of any witnesses should also be recorded if possible.

Risk assessments

Virtually all modern health and safety legislation is based around the concept of risk assessment. You will need to carry out a risk assessment of the churchyard itself, the machinery you use for maintenance and the various activities which are undertaken including fetes and other fundraising activities.

First, you will need to record the hazards that exist. These are features that have the potential to cause harm such as worn steps, slippery paths, chemicals and dangerous machinery. Then look at the risk. This is the likelihood that harm from a particular hazard will be realized. In other words, what is the probability that people will actually fall down the steps, slip on the path or injure themselves with dangerous chemicals or machinery, and if they do what is the severity of the accident likely to be? It could be only minor cuts and scratches or it might possibly be fatal.

You then need to record in each case what control measures you have in place and if any additional controls are necessary. For example, there may be no handrails, in which case the installation of handrails on steps and paths would reduce the risks of slips and falls. You may not have any personal protective equipment for use with chemicals and machinery, in which case the provision of these would be the additional measures you need. Your risk assessments and what you do to reduce the risks need to be recorded. In this way if an accident subsequently happens you can demonstrate that you have done all that is reasonably possible, that you have not been negligent and that you have shown a duty of care as required under the Occupiers' Liability Acts.

Faculties

Frequent reference is made elsewhere to the need to obtain the appropriate faculty and planning permission for any work undertaken in the churchyard. The same rules apply to any work required for health and safety matters. However, where there is a serious risk of injury, for example falling masonry or the appearance of a large hole in the churchyard, immediate reversible measures such as fencing off and the erection of warning signs must be carried out to make the area safe. Archdeacons should be consulted, who should be able to approve an emergency order for this temporary work. The appropriate procedures can then be followed regarding the permanent work that needs to be undertaken.

Notes

chapter 2

1 Church of England Assembly (Powers) Act 1919, Section 4 and Synodical Government Measure 1969, Section 2(1).

2 Care of Churches and Ecclesiastical Jurisdiction Measure 1991, Section 2 and Schedules 1 and 2.

3 Parochial Church Councils (Powers) Measure 1956, Section 2 (as substituted by Synodical Government Measure 1969, Section 6) and Section 4.

4 Faculty Jurisdiction Measure 1964, Section 7.

5 *Re West Norwood Cemetery* [1994], Fam 211.

6 Faculty Jurisdiction Rules 1992 (SI No. 2882) rule 6 and Appendix A, paragraph 4.

7 Ancient Monuments and Archaeological Areas Act 1979, Sections 1 and 61(7).

8 *Ibid*, Section 61(8).

9 Wildlife and Countryside Act 1981, Section 28.

10 *Ibid*, Section 29.

11 Town and Country Planning Act 1990, Part VIII.

12 *Re Plumstead Burial Ground* [1895] P 225.

13 Wildlife and Countryside Act 1981, Section 53.

14 Highways Act 1980, Sections 118, 119; also Road Traffic Regulations Act 1984 Part II, as amended by Road Traffic (Temporary Restrictions) Act 1991.

15 Highways Act 1980, Section 31.

16 *Re St Mary's Aldermary* [1985] Fam 101. If a way leave is granted to neighbouring properties, as with rights of access on foot, or for vehicles, it would seem that the faculty will only create a licence and not an irrevocable right. It will normally be for a set time and, if it is open-ended, it will probably be revocable on reasonable notice.

17 *Re All Saints, Harborough Magna* [1992] 4 All ER 948.

18 Endowments and Glebe Measure 1976, Section 20 and Parsonages Measure 1938, Section 1.

19 *St Edmundsbury and Ipswich Diocesan Board of Finance v Clark* (No. 2) [1975] 1 WLR 468.

20 Canon F 13.2.

21 *Wringe v Cohen* [1940] 1KB 229.

22 *Re St Peter and St Paul, Scrayingham* [1991] 4 All ER 411.

23   Limitation Act 1980, Sections 15 and 17.

24   Inspection of Churches Measure 1955, as amended by Care of Churches and Ecclesiastical Jurisdiction Measure 1991, Schedule 3.

25   Parochial Church Councils (Powers) Measure 1956, Section 4(1)(ii)(c).

26   Occupiers' Liability Act 1957, Section 2.

27   Occupiers' Liability Act 1984, Section 1(5).

28   Canon F 13.2.

29   *Tarry v Ashton* (1876) 1 QBD 314;

30   *R v Farrant* [1973] Crim LR 240.

chapter 3

1   Public Health (Control of Disease) Act 1984, Section 46.

2   Local Government Act 1972, Section 214.

3   Church of England (Miscellaneous Provisions) Measure 1976, Section 6(1), as amended by Church of England (Miscellaneous Provisions) Measure 1992, Section 17 and Schedule 3, paragraph 12. See too the 1992 Measure, Section 3.

4   Church Representation Rules contained in the Synodical Government Measure 1969, Section 7 and Schedule 3 rule 1(2).

5   Church of England (Miscellaneous Provisions) Measure 1976, Section 6(2).

6   Parochial Church Councils (Powers) Measure 1956, Section 4(1)(ii)(c).

7   Church of England (Miscellaneous Provisions) Measure 1976, Section 6(2).

8   *Re West Pennard Churchyard* [1991] 4 All ER 124; *Re St Mary's Churchyard, Alderley* [1994] 1 WLR 1478.

9   Town Improvement Clauses Act 1847, Section 103.

10   *Re St Lukes, Holbeach Hurn, Watson v Howard* [1990] 2 All ER 749.

11   Consecration of Churchyards Act 1867 and Consecration of Churchyards Act 1868.

12   Canon B 38, paragraph 4(b).

13   Church of England (Miscellaneous Provisions) Measure 1992, Section 3.

14   Since the Public Health Act 1848.

15   *Re St Peter's Folkestone* [1982] 1 WLR 1283.

16   Burial Act 1853, Section 4.

17   Church of England (Miscellaneous Provisions) Measure 1992, Section 3(1).

18   Faculty Jurisdiction Rules 1992 (SI 1992 No.2882) rule 12.

19   Coroners' Act 1988, Section 23.

20   Burial Act 1857, Section 25.

21   *Re Christchurch, Alsager* [1999] 1 All ER 117, Chancery Court of York.

22   *Re Atkins* [1989] 1 All ER 14; *Re Church Norton Churchyard* [1989] Fam 37; *Re St Peter's Church, Oughtrington* [1993] 1 WLR 1440; *Re St Mary's Churchyard, Alderley* [1994] 1 WLR 1478.

23   *Re West Norwood Cemetery* [1994] Fam 210.

chapter 4

1   Cf *Re St Luke's, Holbeach Hurn* [1990] 2 All ER 749.

2   Care of Churches and Ecclesiastical Jurisdiction Measure 1991, Section 13. See too, Faculty Jurisdiction (Injunctions and Restoration Orders) Rules 1992 (SI 1992 No.2884).

3   Ecclesiastical Jurisdiction Measure 1963, Sections 60 and 61.

4   *Re Woldingham Churchyard* [1957] 1 WLR 811.

5   Ecclesiastical Jurisdiction Measure 1963, Section 81, as amended by the Care of Churches and Ecclesiastical Jurisdiction Measure 1991, Schedule 4, paragraph 11.

6   Care of Churches and Ecclesiastical Jurisdiction Measure 1991, Section 15.

7   *Re St Mark's Haydock* (No.2) [1981] 1 WLR 1167.

8   *Re Holy Trinity Churchyard, Freckleton* [1995] 1 WLR 1588.

9   *Re St Chad's Churchyard, Bishop's Tachbrook* [1993] 1 All ER 208.

chapter 5

1   Parochial Church Councils (Powers) Measure 1956, especially Section 2 (as substituted by Synodical Government Measure 1969) and Section 4.

2   Parochial Registers and Records Measure 1978 as amended by Church of England (Miscellaneous Provisions) Measure 1992.

3   *Ibid*, Section 1(2).

4   *Ibid*, Section 6(1).

5   *Ibid*, Section 6(2).

6   Parochial Registers and Records Measure 1978, Sections 1 and 3. Also Church of England (Miscellaneous Provisions) Measure 1992, Schedule 1, paragraphs 10 and 11.

7   *Ibid*, Schedule 1, form no. 2.

8   Care of Churches and Ecclesiastical Jurisdiction Measure 1991, Section 4(1).

9   *Ibid*, s. 4(3). The Council for the Care of Churches has produced standard forms in *Church Property Register and Church Log Book*, published by Church House Publishing.

10   *Ibid*, Sections 5(3) and (4).

11   *Ibid*, Section 5(1)(a) and (3).

12   *Ibid*, Sections 4(2) and 5(2).

13   Inspection of Churches Measure 1955, as amended by Care of Churches and Ecclesiastical Jurisdiction Measure 1991, Schedule 3.

14   Inspection of Churches Measure 1955, Section 1A(c).

15   *Ibid*, Section 1A(b) and Section 6.

16   Parochial Registers and Records Measure 1978, Sections 1 and 3.

17   Care of Churches and Ecclesiastical Jurisdiction Measure 1991, Section 11(8).

18   *Ibid*, Section 14 and Faculty Jurisdiction Rules 1992 (SI No. 2882) rule 6 and Appendix A.

19   SI 1992 (No. 2882) rules 6(3) and 7.

20   *Ibid*, rule 7.

21   Legal Advisory Commission *Legal Opinions Concerning the Church of England*, 1994, London, 66.

22   Refuse Disposal (Amenity) Act 1978, Section 2.

23   *Ibid*, Sections 3 and 6.

24   Environmental Protection Act 1990, Sections 89 and 90. The local authority is normally the District Council. In London, it is the Common Council of the City or the council of the relevant London Borough.

25   Faculty Jurisdiction Rules 1992 (SI No. 2882) rule 6 and Appendix A, paragraph 4(iv).

26   Care of Churches and Ecclesiastical Jurisdiction Measure 1991, Section 6 as amended by the Church of England (Miscellaneous Provisions) Measure 1995, Section 13.

27   *Ibid*, Section 6(3).

28   *Ibid*, Section 6(5).

29   *Ibid*, Section 6(1).

30   *Ibid*, Section 6(2).

31   Town and Country Planning Act 1990, Section 211 ff.

32   *Ibid*, Section 197 ff.

33   *Ibid*, Section 210.

34   *Ibid*, Section 206.

35   *Ibid*, Section 198(6).

36   *Ibid*, Section 211.

37   Care of Churches and Ecclesiastical Jurisdiction Measure 1991, Section 7.

38   Currently fees are set by Parochial Fees Order 2000 (SI No. 2049).

39   Charities Act 1993, Part VI and General Synod Church Accounting Regulations 1997.

40   Local Government Act 1972, Section 214 (1) and (8) and Schedule 26.

41   *Ibid*, Section 215.

42   Open Spaces Act 1906, Section 9(b).

43   Parish Councils and Burial Authorities (Miscellaneous Provisions) Act 1970, Section 1.

44   Local Government Act 1972, Section 214(6) and (8).

45   In Wales a County or County Borough; Local Government (Wales) Act 1994, Schedule 15.

46   Local Government Act 1972, Section 214(1).

47   National Heritage Act 1980, Section 3, as substituted by the National Heritage Act 1997.

48   Ancient Monuments and Archaeological Areas Act 1979, Section 24(4) and (2) (as amended by National Heritage Act 1983, Schedule 4, paragraph 48).

49   War Memorials (Local Authorities) Powers Act 1923, Section 1, as amended by Local Government Act 1948, Section 133(1) and (2).

50   Parish Councils Act 1957, Sections 1, 2 and 3. For clocks see also Public Health Act 1875, Section 165, as extended by Public Health Amendment Act 1890, Section 46.

51   Inner Urban Areas Act 1978, Section 5.

chapter 6

1   Town and Country Planning Act 1990, Section 76.

2   Disability Discrimination Act 1995, Section 19.

3   Department of National Heritage *The Treasure Act 1996 Code of Practice (England and Wales)* 1997, paragraph 16. Now available from the DCMS.

4   Faculty Jurisdiction Rules 1992 (SI No. 2882) rule 12, cf rule 5.

5   Open Spaces Act 1906, Section 9(b).

6   *Ibid*, Section 10.

7   Local Government Act 1972, Section 215(1).

8   *Ibid*, Section 215(2).

9   *Ibid*, Section 214(1) and (8) and Schedule 26, and Local Authorities, etc. (Miscellaneous Provisions) Order 1974 (SI 482), Articles 15 and 16.

10   *Re St Michael and All Angels, Tettenhall Regis* [1995] Fam 179 and 190A and *Re St Mary's, Barnes* [1982] 1 WLR 531.

11   Church of England (Miscellaneous Provisions) Measure 1992, Section 3(1).

12   Home Office *Notes on Orders requiring the discontinuance of burials in Church of England Church Yards*.

13   Burial Act 1853, Section 1. See too Local Government Act 1972, Section 272 and Schedules 26 (paragraph 15) and 30. There are a few churchyards where the power to make an Order in Council under the 1853 Act may not apply, particularly

ones that were set up under specific Acts of Parliament. See here Legal Advisory
Commission *Legal Opinions concerning the Church of England*, 1994, London, 61.

14   Consecration of Churchyards Acts 1867, Section 11.

15   *Legal Opinions Concerning the Church of England, supra 1.*

16   Disused Burial Grounds Act 1884, Section 3.

17   *Re St Michael and All Angels, Tettenhall Regis* [1995] Fam 179.

18   Pastoral Measure 1983, Sections 30(4) and 51(11).

19   *Ibid*, Section 28.

20   *Ibid*, Section 2.

21   *Ibid*, Sections 3 – 8.

22   *Ibid*, Section 9.

23   *Ibid*, Sections 28 and 51.

24   *Ibid*, Section 30(1).

25   *Ibid*, Section 30(2).

26   *Ibid*, Section 30(3).

27   *Ibid*, Section 47(2) or Section 51(1)(6) as amended by Pastoral (Amendment)
      Measure 1994, Sections 3 and 4.

28   Pastoral (Amendment) Measure 1994, Section 13.

29   Pastoral Measure 1983, Section 47(3).

30   *Ibid*, Sections 49 or 51(1)(c).

31   *Ibid*, Sections 46(1)(a), 47(1) or 49(1)(i) or (ii) and 51(2) and (3).

32   *Ibid,* Sections 51(2)(a) and (3).

33   *Ibid*, Section 51(3)(b).

34   *Ibid*, Section 61 and Section 30(5).

35   *Ibid*, Section 59(7).

36   *Ibid*, Section 65(3).

37   *Ibid*, Schedule 6, Articles 1 and 2.

38   *Ibid*, Schedule 6, Article 7.

39   *Ibid*, Schedule 6, Article 3.

40   *Ibid*, Schedule 6, Articles 4, 5 and 6.

41   *Ibid*, Schedule 6, Article 9.

42   *Ibid*, Schedule 6, Article 10.

43   *Ibid*, Schedule 6, Article 11.

44   Town and Country Planning Act 1990, Sections 55 and 57.

45   Consecration of Churchyards Act 1867, Section 9, as amended by the
      Consecration of Churchyards Act 1868, Section 1.

46   Endowments and Glebe Measure 1976, Section 20 as amended by Church of England (Miscellaneous Provisions) Measure 1992 Section 17(1) and Schedule 3, para. 15, and New Parishes Measure 1943, Section 17, as substituted by Church Property (Miscellaneous Provisions) Measure 1960, Section 6(2) as amended by Church of England (Miscellaneous Provisions) Measure 1992 Section 8(b).

47   Local Authorities Cemeteries Order 1977, (SI 1977, No.204), Article 5(4).

48   Local Government Act 1972, Section 214(2).

49   *Ibid*, Section 121.

50   Places of Worship Sites Act 1873, Section 1 and Places of Worship Sites Amendment Act 1882, Section 1.

51   Local Government Act 1972, Sections 123 and 127 as amended by Local Government Planning and Land Act 1980 Schedule 23, Part V.

52   *Re St John's Church, Bishop's Hatfield* [1967] P. 113.

53   Faculty Jurisdiction Measure 1964, Section 7(1).

54   Local Authorities Cemetery Order 1977 (SI 1977, No. 204), Article 5.

55   *Re Atkins* [1989] 1 All ER 14 and *Re West Norwood Cemetery* [1994] Fam 210.

56   Local Authorities Cemeteries Order 1977 (SI No. 204) and see *Re Coleford Cemetery* [1984] 1 WLR 1369; *Re St Andrew's, North Weald Bassett* [1987] 1 WLR 1503; *Re St John's Chelsea* [1962] 1 WLR 706.

appendix 2

1   *Charity and Voluntary Workers – A Guide to Health and Safety at Work*, HSE Books, PO Box 1999, Sudbury, Suffolk.

2   Institute of Burial and Cremation Administration Inc., *Code of Safe Working Practice for Cemeteries*, 1999.

Further reading, bibliography and useful addresses

The Council for the Care of Churches is able to offer advice on all aspects of churchyard management and holds a register of craftspeople who can undertake the design and carving of grave markers. The Council's offices are at Church House, Great Smith Street, London SW1P 3NZ. Email: enquiries@c-of-e.org.uk

At a local level, your Diocesan Advisory Committee for the Care of Churches will also be able to offer help and advice on the topics covered by this book.

The legal framework

Dale, William   *The Law of the Parish Church* (Seventh Edition), Butterworths, 1998

Doe, Norman   *The Legal Framework of the Church of England*, Clarendon Press, 1996

Leeder, Lynne   *Ecclesiastical Law handbook*, Sweet and Maxwell, 1997

Newsom, G. H. and Newsom, G. L.   *Faculty Jurisdiction of the Church of England* (Second Edition), Sweet and Maxwell, London, 1993

A Guide to Church Inspection and Repair, Church House Publishing, 1995

The National Amenity Societies, Council for the Care of Churches, 1998

Commissioning a memorial

Frazer, H.   *Memorials by Artists*, Saxmundham, 1998

Memorials by Artists, Snape Priory, Snape, Saxmundham, Suffolk IP17 1SA

The National Association of Memorial Masons,
27a Albert Street, Rugby, Warwickshire CV21 2SG

The Crafts Council, 44a Pentonville Road, London
N1 9BY

The archaeology and history of the churchyard

Blair, J. and   *Church Archaeology: Research Directions*
Pyrah, C. (eds)   *for the Future*, CBA, 1996

Cocke, Thomas   *Recording a Church: An Illustrated Glossary*,
Finley, Donald   CBA, 1996
Halsey, Richard and
Williamson, Elizabeth

Lees, Hilary   *English Churchyard Memorials*, Tempus
                     Publishing, 2000

Mytum, Harold   *Recording and Analysing Graveyards*, CBA,
                     2000

Council for the Care   *Church Archaeology, its Care and Management*,
of Churches of the   unpublished report, 1997, available from the
Church of England   Council for the Care of Churches, 1997

The Council for British Archaeology, Bowes
Morrell House, 111 Walmgate, York YO1 2UA

The Society for Church Archaeology, c/o
CBA, Bowes Morrell House, 111 Walmgate,
York YO1 2UA

The living churchyard

The Council for the Care of Churches (address above) holds a comprehensive
list prepared by Revd Nigel Cooper of the relevant publications and organizations
in this field. Below are a few of the key titles.

Biddle, Giles   *Tree Root Damage to Buildings*, Atlantic
                     Books, 1997

Cooper, Nigel   *Wildlife in Church and Churchyard: Plants,*
Animals and their Management, 2nd edn, Church
House Publishing (for the Council for the
Care of Churches), 2001

Deane-Drummond,   *A Handbook in Theology and Ecology,* SCM Press,
     Celia   1996

Hill, David A. and   *Managing Habitats for Conservation,* Cambridge
Sutherland, William J.   University Press, 1995
     (eds)

Lonsdale, David   *Principles of Tree Assessment and Management,*
The Stationery Office, 1998

Parker, Mary   *The Living Churchyard,* Community Service
Volunteers, 1989: a DIY pack, available from the
Living Churchyard Project, The Arthur Rank Centre,
National Agricultural Centre, Stoneleigh Park,
Warwickshire CV8 2LZ
This is the hub of churchyard conservation with a
network of contacts, and holds many useful leaflets.

The Recognition of Hazardous Trees, leaflet from the
Forestry Authority

Veteran Trees: A guide to Risk and Responsibility,
English Nature, 2000

Index